WEEKEND SIDE HUSTLE TECHNIQUES:
AFTER 5 to 9, HOW TO MAKE MONEY ON THE SIDE IN YOUR SPARE TIME

BY
HENRY E. PARKINS

TABLE OF CONTENTS

COPYRIGHT PAGE   2

TABLE OF CONTENTS   3

INTRODUCTION   7

Overview: The Growing Trend of Side Hustles   10

Importance of Utilizing Spare Time for Additional Income   13

Purpose of the Book   17

CHAPTER 1   20

UNDERSTANDING SIDE HUSTLES   20

Definition and Significance of Side Hustles   24

Differentiating Between Full-Time Jobs and Side Hustles   28

Benefits of Engaging in Side Hustles   31

CHAPTER 2   36

IDENTIFYING YOUR SKILLS AND INTERESTS   36

Self-Assessment of Skills, Talents, and Interests   40

Identifying Marketable Skills and Hobbies   44

Understanding the Potential for Monetizing Skills and Interests   49

3

Identifying Marketable Skills and Talents — 50

CHAPTER 3 — 55

WEEKEND SIDE HUSTLE IDEAS — 55

Overview of Various Side Hustle Opportunities — 59

Exploring Freelance Work and Gig Economy Platforms — 65

Leveraging Online Marketplaces for Selling Products or Services — 69

Exploring Offline Opportunities and Local Markets — 74

Evaluating the Feasibility and Profitability of Different Ideas — 79

CHAPTER 4 — 83

TIME MANAGEMENT STRATEGIES — 83

Balancing Full-Time Commitments with Side Hustle Endeavors — 88

Creating a Structured Schedule for Side Hustle Activities — 93

Prioritizing Tasks and Maximizing Productivity During Spare Time — 98

CHAPTER 5 — 104

FINANCIAL PLANNING AND INVESTMENT — 104

Setting Financial Goals for Side Hustle Income — 106

Budgeting and Managing Expenses Effectively — 112

Investing Profits for Long-Term Financial Stability — 117

CHAPTER 6 — 123

MARKETING AND PROMOTION   123

Building a Personal Brand for Side Hustle Ventures   130

Utilizing Social Media and Online Marketing Channels   135

Networking and Forming Partnerships for Business Growth   141

CHAPTER 7   147

OVERCOMING CHALLENGES AND OBSTACLES   147

Addressing Common Challenges Faced by Side Hustlers   153

Strategies for Managing Stress and Burnout   159

Learning from Failures and Adapting to Setbacks   164

CHAPTER 8   169

LEGAL AND REGULATORY CONSIDERATIONS   169

Understanding Legal Requirements for Side Businesses   174

Registering a Business Entity and Obtaining Necessary Licenses   179

Complying with Tax Regulations and Financial Reporting Obligations   183

CHAPTER 9   188

SCALING YOUR SIDE HUSTLE   188

Strategies for Expanding and Diversifying Side Hustle Ventures   193

Hiring Assistance and Delegating Tasks as the Business Grows   199

Maintaining Work-Life Balance While Scaling Operations   204

CHAPTER 10   209

CONCLUSION: EMBRACING THE JOURNEY OF FINANCIAL EMPOWERMENT   209

Recap of Key Insights and Strategies   213

Encouragement for Readers to Take Action and Pursue Their Side Hustle Goals   217

Final Thoughts on the Significance of Leveraging Spare Time for Financial Empowerment   220

INTRODUCTION

In today's fast-paced world, where demands on our time seem to be ever-expanding, the concept of the side hustle has emerged as a beacon of opportunity. As the traditional nine-to-five work model evolves, more and more individuals are seeking ways to leverage their spare time outside of regular employment to generate additional income and pursue their passions. It is within this context that "Weekend Side Hustle Techniques: After 5 to 9, How to Make Money on the Side in Your Spare Time" emerges as a practical guide and companion for those eager to unlock the potential of their free hours.

This book is a roadmap for the modern entrepreneur, the ambitious dreamer, and the everyday individual seeking to augment their income,

7

explore new avenues of creativity, or simply gain greater financial freedom. Whether you aspire to turn a hobby into a thriving business, explore freelance opportunities, or dip your toes into the vast sea of the gig economy, "Weekend Side Hustle Techniques" is designed to equip you with the knowledge, tools, and inspiration needed to succeed.

Within these pages, you will find a treasure trove of strategies, insights, and actionable steps to help you navigate the world of side hustles with confidence and clarity. From identifying your unique skills and interests to managing your time effectively, from marketing your offerings to scaling your ventures, this book covers every aspect of the side hustle journey.

But more than just a practical manual, "Weekend Side Hustle

Techniques" is a testament to the power of ambition, resilience, and the unwavering belief that a brighter future is within reach for those willing to pursue it. It is a celebration of the entrepreneurial spirit that resides within each of us, waiting to be unleashed and nurtured.

As you embark on this journey, remember that your spare time is not merely a commodity to be spent, but a canvas upon which you can paint the picture of your dreams. With dedication, perseverance, and the guidance offered in these pages, you have the potential to transform your weekends and evenings into a source of fulfillment, purpose, and prosperity.

So, whether you are a seasoned entrepreneur or a novice explorer of the business world, let "Weekend Side Hustle Techniques" be your trusted companion as you embark on this exhilarating adventure. Your journey towards financial independence and personal empowerment starts here.

Overview: The Growing Trend of Side Hustles

The concept of side hustles is explored as a burgeoning trend that reflects the shifting landscape of work and entrepreneurship in the modern world. The overview of this growing trend serves as a foundational understanding for readers, contextualizing the importance and relevance of pursuing additional income streams outside of traditional employment.

Changing Nature of Work: The traditional nine-to-five work model is no longer the sole paradigm for earning a living. With advancements in technology, changes in consumer behavior, and the rise of the gig economy, individuals are increasingly seeking alternative ways to generate income and pursue their passions.

Economic Pressures: In today's economy, many individuals face financial pressures and challenges such as rising living costs, stagnant wages, and job insecurity. Side hustles offer a means to supplement income, alleviate financial strain, and achieve greater financial stability.

Flexibility and Autonomy: Side hustles provide individuals with the flexibility and autonomy to create their own schedules, pursue their interests, and explore entrepreneurial ventures without the constraints of traditional employment. This freedom empowers

11

individuals to design their work-life balance according to their preferences and priorities.

Entrepreneurial Spirit: The rise of side hustles reflects the entrepreneurial spirit inherent in many individuals. Whether driven by a desire for financial independence, a passion for creativity, or a pursuit of personal fulfillment, side hustles enable individuals to channel their entrepreneurial aspirations into tangible ventures and opportunities.

Diversification of Income: In an uncertain economic climate, diversifying income streams through side hustles can provide a safety net against unexpected financial challenges and disruptions. By leveraging multiple sources of income, individuals can build resilience and mitigate risks

12

associated with relying solely on a single source of revenue.

Technological Advancements: The proliferation of digital platforms, online marketplaces, and social media channels has democratized access to entrepreneurship and enabled individuals to reach global audiences with minimal barriers to entry. This democratization of entrepreneurship has paved the way for the widespread adoption of side hustles as a viable means of income generation.

Importance of Utilizing Spare Time for Additional Income

The importance of utilizing spare time for additional income is emphasized as a strategic approach to achieving financial goals, pursuing personal passions, and unlocking greater opportunities for economic empowerment. Several key reasons underscore the significance of leveraging spare time for income generation:

Financial Freedom: Utilizing spare time for additional income provides individuals with the opportunity to achieve financial freedom and independence. By diversifying income streams and supplementing earnings from primary sources, individuals can build a stronger financial foundation, reduce financial stress, and gain greater control over their financial futures.

Maximizing Productivity: Spare time represents untapped potential for productivity and growth. By harnessing spare moments, evenings, and weekends effectively, individuals can capitalize on otherwise idle time and channel it towards activities that generate tangible returns. Through strategic time management and prioritization, spare time can be transformed into valuable opportunities for personal and professional advancement.

Pursuing Passion Projects: Side hustles enable individuals to pursue their passions, interests, and creative endeavors outside of traditional employment. By monetizing hobbies, talents, and skills, individuals can derive fulfillment and satisfaction from their work, turning leisure activities into sources of income and personal fulfillment.

Creating Opportunities for Growth: Spare time presents a valuable opportunity for individuals to explore new avenues of growth, learning, and skill development. By investing time and energy into side

15

hustle ventures, individuals can acquire new skills, expand their knowledge base, and cultivate entrepreneurial acumen, ultimately enhancing their employability and marketability in an ever-evolving job market.

Building Resilience: In an increasingly volatile and unpredictable economy, diversifying income sources through side hustles can help individuals build resilience against economic downturns, job loss, and unforeseen financial challenges. By spreading risk across multiple income streams, individuals can mitigate the impact of setbacks and disruptions, ensuring greater stability and security over the long term.

Unlocking Entrepreneurial Potential: Side hustles serve as a gateway to entrepreneurship, allowing individuals to test business ideas, validate market demand, and gain hands-on experience in running a business. By starting small and gradually scaling operations, individuals can unleash their entrepreneurial potential, explore innovative business models, and pursue opportunities for growth and expansion.

Purpose of the Book

The purpose of "Weekend Side Hustle Techniques: After 5 to 9, How to Make Money on the Side in Your Spare Time" is to empower individuals with the knowledge, strategies, and resources needed to harness the potential of their spare time for additional income generation and personal fulfillment. The book is designed to serve as a comprehensive guide and roadmap for readers seeking to explore, launch, and grow successful side hustle ventures outside of their primary employment. The key purposes of the book include:

Inspiring Action: The book aims to inspire readers to take proactive steps towards achieving their financial goals and pursuing their passions. By sharing real-world examples, success stories, and actionable insights, the book seeks to motivate readers to leverage their spare time as a catalyst for positive change and personal growth.

Providing Practical Guidance: "Weekend Side Hustle Techniques" offers practical, hands-on guidance for every stage of the side hustle journey, from idea generation and validation to implementation, management, and growth. Through actionable tips, strategies, and exercises, readers are equipped with the tools and resources needed to navigate the complexities of starting and running a successful side hustle.

Fostering Entrepreneurial Mindset: The book aims to cultivate an entrepreneurial mindset among readers, encouraging them to think creatively, embrace uncertainty, and seize opportunities for innovation and growth. By instilling principles of resilience, adaptability, and resourcefulness, the book empowers readers to overcome challenges, learn from failures, and persevere in the pursuit of their goals.

Promoting Financial Empowerment: At its core, "Weekend Side Hustle Techniques" is about promoting financial empowerment and independence. By diversifying income streams, maximizing productivity, and investing in personal and professional development, readers are empowered to take control of their financial futures, build wealth, and achieve greater financial security and stability.

Encouraging Work-Life Balance: The book emphasizes the importance of maintaining a healthy work-life balance while pursuing side hustle ventures. By providing practical strategies for time management, stress reduction, and self-care, readers are encouraged to prioritize their well-being and establish sustainable habits that support both their personal and professional aspirations.

CHAPTER 1

UNDERSTANDING SIDE HUSTLES

Understanding side hustles forms the foundational knowledge necessary for readers to embark on their journey towards supplemental income and personal fulfillment. This section delves into the multifaceted nature of side hustles, offering insights into their definition, significance, and distinct characteristics.

Definition of Side Hustles: The book begins by defining side hustles as supplementary income-generating activities pursued outside of one's primary employment. Unlike traditional full-time jobs, side hustles are characterized by their flexibility, autonomy, and entrepreneurial spirit.

21

They encompass a wide range of endeavors, including freelance work, online businesses, gig economy opportunities, and creative ventures.

Significance of Side Hustles: Understanding the significance of side hustles is essential for readers to appreciate their role in modern-day economics and personal finance. Side hustles offer individuals the opportunity to diversify their income streams, mitigate financial risks, and pursue their passions and interests beyond the confines of traditional employment. They represent a pathway to financial independence, personal fulfillment, and professional growth in an increasingly dynamic and competitive landscape.

Differentiation from Full-Time Employment: It is crucial for readers to distinguish between side hustles and full-time employment to appreciate their unique characteristics and advantages. Unlike traditional jobs, side hustles typically offer greater flexibility, autonomy, and creative freedom. They allow individuals to pursue multiple income streams, explore diverse interests, and balance their professional and personal lives according to their preferences and priorities.

Benefits of Side Hustles: The book highlights the numerous benefits associated with engaging in side hustles. These include the potential for supplemental income generation, skill development, networking opportunities, and personal fulfillment. Side hustles enable individuals to explore new interests, test business ideas, and build valuable experience and expertise that can enhance their employability and marketability in the long term.

Challenges and Considerations:

While side hustles offer myriad opportunities for growth and fulfillment, they also come with unique challenges and considerations. Readers are encouraged to be mindful of potential pitfalls such as time management issues, financial risks, and burnout. By acknowledging these challenges and adopting a proactive approach to addressing them, individuals can navigate the complexities of side hustle ventures more effectively and sustainably.

Definition and Significance of Side Hustles

side hustles are defined as supplementary income-generating activities pursued outside of one's primary employment. They represent a strategic approach to leveraging spare time, skills, and resources to generate additional income, pursue personal passions, and achieve greater financial independence and flexibility.

Definition of Side Hustles: Side hustles encompass a diverse array of income-generating activities that individuals undertake outside of their regular employment. These activities may include freelance work, consulting gigs, online businesses, part-time jobs, creative pursuits, and entrepreneurial ventures. Side hustles are characterized by their flexibility, autonomy, and potential for scalability, allowing individuals to explore diverse interests, talents, and opportunities for income generation.

Significance of Side Hustles: Side hustles play a pivotal role in modern-day economics and personal finance, offering individuals a means to diversify their income streams, supplement their earnings, and pursue their passions beyond the confines of traditional employment. The significance of side hustles lies in their ability to provide financial security, flexibility, and empowerment in an increasingly dynamic and competitive job market. They enable individuals to take control of their financial futures, explore new avenues of growth and innovation, and build valuable skills and experience that enhance their professional and personal development.

Economic Empowerment: Side hustles empower individuals to take ownership of their financial well-being and pursue opportunities for income generation and wealth accumulation. By diversifying income streams and reducing reliance on a single source of income, individuals can mitigate financial risks, weather economic uncertainties, and achieve greater financial resilience and stability over the long term.

Flexibility and Autonomy: Unlike traditional employment, side hustles offer individuals greater flexibility, autonomy, and control over their work schedules, priorities, and career paths. They allow individuals to balance multiple commitments, pursue diverse interests, and tailor their work arrangements to accommodate their lifestyle preferences and personal goals.

Personal Fulfillment: Side hustles provide individuals with a platform to pursue their passions, interests, and creative endeavors outside of their primary employment. Whether it's launching a small business, freelancing in a chosen field, or pursuing a hobby, side hustles enable individuals to derive satisfaction, fulfillment, and a sense of purpose from their work, fostering personal growth, self-discovery, and fulfillment in the process.

Differentiating Between Full-Time Jobs and Side Hustles

it's essential for readers to understand the distinctions between full-time jobs and side hustles. Recognizing these differences is crucial for individuals considering or already engaged in side hustle endeavors. Here are key points of differentiation highlighted in the book:

Employment Status:

Full-time Jobs: Full-time jobs typically involve a formal employment arrangement where individuals work for a single employer on a regular basis, often for 40 hours per week or more. Employees may receive benefits such as health insurance, retirement plans, and paid time off.

Side Hustles: Side hustles are supplementary income-generating activities pursued outside of primary employment. They are often undertaken independently or on a freelance basis, allowing individuals to work on their own terms and schedule.

Time Commitment:

Full-time Jobs: Full-time jobs require a significant time commitment, with employees devoting the majority of their weekdays to work-related

29

responsibilities during standard business hours.

Side Hustles: Side hustles are typically pursued during individuals' spare time outside of their primary work hours, such as evenings, weekends, or other non-traditional hours. They offer flexibility in scheduling and can be tailored to fit around existing commitments.

Income Generation:

Full-time Jobs: Full-time jobs serve as the primary source of income for individuals, providing a steady paycheck and financial stability.

Side Hustles: Side hustles supplement primary income by generating additional revenue streams. While they may not initially provide the same level of income as full-time employment, successful side hustles have the potential to grow into lucrative ventures over time.

Purpose and Motivation:

Full-time Jobs: Full-time jobs are often pursued to fulfill career aspirations, meet financial obligations, and build professional expertise and stability.

Side Hustles: Side hustles are driven by a variety of motivations, including the desire for financial independence, the pursuit of creative interests, and the opportunity to explore entrepreneurial ventures outside of traditional employment.

Risk and Stability:

Full-time Jobs: Full-time jobs offer a sense of stability and predictability, with steady income, benefits, and opportunities for career advancement.

Side Hustles: Side hustles involve inherent risks and uncertainties associated with entrepreneurship, including variable income, market fluctuations, and the challenges of building and sustaining a business.

Benefits of Engaging in Side Hustles

The book emphasizes the numerous advantages and benefits associated with engaging in side hustles. By exploring these benefits, readers gain insight into the transformative potential of side hustles in their lives. Here are key benefits highlighted in the book:

Supplemental Income: One of the primary benefits of engaging in side hustles is the opportunity to supplement primary income. Side hustles provide individuals with additional revenue streams, allowing them to increase their earning potential, achieve financial goals, and improve their overall financial well-being.

Flexibility and Autonomy: Side hustles offer individuals greater flexibility and autonomy in how they work and manage their time. Unlike traditional nine-to-five jobs, side hustles can be pursued on a part-time basis, during evenings, weekends, or other non-traditional hours, allowing individuals to balance work with other commitments and responsibilities.

Pursuing Passions and Interests: Side hustles enable individuals to pursue their passions, interests, and hobbies outside of their primary employment. Whether it's starting a small business, freelancing in a creative field, or monetizing a hobby, side hustles provide avenues for

personal fulfillment, creativity, and self-expression.

Skill Development and Growth: Engaging in side hustles offers opportunities for skill development, learning, and personal growth. Individuals can acquire new skills, expand their knowledge base, and gain hands-on experience in areas such as entrepreneurship, marketing, finance, and customer service, enhancing their professional and personal development.

Diversification of Income: Side hustles help individuals diversify their income sources, reducing reliance on a single source of income and mitigating financial risks associated with job loss or economic downturns. By spreading income across multiple streams, individuals can build resilience and stability in their financial lives.

Entrepreneurial Experience: Side hustles provide a platform for individuals to gain entrepreneurial experience and explore business ideas in a low-risk environment. By starting and running a side hustle, individuals develop valuable entrepreneurial skills such as problem-solving, decision-making, and resource management, laying the groundwork for future business endeavors.

Networking and Opportunities: Engaging in side hustles opens doors to new networking opportunities, collaborations, and partnerships. Individuals interact with diverse communities, customers, and stakeholders, expanding their professional network and uncovering potential avenues for growth, collaboration, and career advancement.

Work-Life Balance: Side hustles promote a healthier work-life balance by allowing individuals to pursue their passions, interests, and personal priorities outside of traditional employment. By integrating side hustles into their lives, individuals can achieve greater fulfillment, satisfaction, and harmony between work and personal life.

CHAPTER 2

IDENTIFYING YOUR SKILLS AND INTERESTS

The process of identifying your skills and interests forms a foundational step in discovering lucrative and fulfilling side hustle opportunities. By recognizing and leveraging your unique talents and passions, you can maximize the potential for success and satisfaction in your entrepreneurial endeavors. Here's how the book guides readers through this process:

Self-Assessment: The book encourages readers to conduct a comprehensive self-assessment to identify their strengths, weaknesses, interests, and areas of expertise. This involves reflecting on past experiences, achievements, and hobbies, as well as considering personal preferences, values, and aspirations. Through introspection and self-awareness, readers gain valuable insights into their skills, interests, and potential avenues for side hustle exploration.

Skills Inventory: Readers are prompted to create a skills inventory outlining their core competencies, professional qualifications, and specialized knowledge areas. This inventory may include technical skills, soft skills, industry expertise, and creative talents that can be leveraged in side hustle ventures. By cataloging their skills and competencies, readers gain clarity on their unique value proposition and potential opportunities for monetization.

Passion Mapping: The book guides readers through a process of passion mapping to identify their interests, hobbies, and areas of personal fulfillment. This involves brainstorming activities, subjects, and pursuits that bring joy, fulfillment, and a sense of purpose. By exploring their passions and interests, readers uncover potential side hustle ideas that align with their values, preferences, and aspirations.

Market Research: In addition to self-assessment, the book emphasizes the importance of conducting market research to identify viable side hustle opportunities. This involves analyzing market trends, consumer preferences, competition, and demand for products or services within chosen niches. By understanding market dynamics and identifying unmet needs or underserved audiences, readers can tailor their side hustle ventures to address specific market gaps and opportunities.

SWOT Analysis: Readers are encouraged to perform a SWOT analysis (Strengths, Weaknesses, Opportunities, Threats) to evaluate the viability and potential challenges of their side hustle ideas. This strategic assessment helps readers identify areas of competitive advantage, potential obstacles, and areas for improvement. By leveraging their strengths, mitigating weaknesses, and capitalizing on opportunities, readers can enhance the success and sustainability of their side hustle ventures.

Feedback and Iteration: The book emphasizes the importance of seeking feedback from mentors, peers, and potential customers to validate side hustle ideas and refine business concepts. By soliciting input and iterating on their ideas based on feedback, readers can strengthen their value proposition, improve product-market fit, and increase the likelihood of success in their side hustle endeavors.

Self-Assessment of Skills, Talents, and Interests

Conducting a thorough self-assessment of skills, talents, and interests serves as a critical first step in identifying lucrative and fulfilling side hustle opportunities. By introspecting and evaluating personal strengths, weaknesses, and passions, individuals can uncover potential avenues for entrepreneurial exploration. Here's how the book guides readers through this process:

Skills Inventory:

Identify Technical Skills: Consider your proficiency in technical areas such as computer programming, graphic design, writing, photography, marketing, customer service, or data analysis.

Assess Soft Skills: Reflect on your interpersonal skills, communication abilities, problem-solving capabilities, time management, adaptability, leadership potential, and ability to work under pressure.

Evaluate Industry Expertise: Determine your level of expertise and experience in specific industries or domains, such as technology, healthcare, finance, education, or creative arts.

Talents and Creative Abilities:

Explore Creative Talents: Reflect on your creative talents and abilities, including artistic skills, musical talents, writing abilities, crafting skills, or other forms of creative expression.

Consider Specialized Knowledge: Identify areas where you possess specialized knowledge or expertise, such as hobbies, interests, or niche subjects that you are passionate about.

Assess Problem-Solving Skills: Evaluate your ability to identify problems, think critically, and develop innovative solutions. Consider instances where you have demonstrated resourcefulness, creativity, and analytical thinking.

Interests and Passions:

Reflect on Hobbies and Interests: Consider activities, hobbies, and interests that bring you joy, fulfillment, and a sense of purpose. Explore topics or pursuits that you are passionate about and enjoy spending time on.

Identify Personal Values: Reflect on your personal values, beliefs, and principles that guide your life and decision-making process. Consider how your values align with potential side hustle opportunities and ventures.

Explore New Opportunities: Be open to exploring new interests, hobbies, and opportunities that you may not have considered before. Embrace curiosity and a willingness to experiment with different ideas and ventures.

Feedback and Reflection:

Seek Feedback: Solicit feedback from mentors, friends, family members, and colleagues who know you well. Ask for their perspectives on your strengths, talents, and areas for development.

Reflect on Past Experiences: Consider past experiences, achievements, successes, and challenges that have shaped your skills, talents, and interests. Reflect on lessons learned and insights gained from previous endeavors.

Iterate and Refine: Continuously iterate and refine your self-assessment based on feedback and reflection. Be open to learning and growth, and be willing to adapt your self-perception as you gain new experiences and insights.

Identifying Marketable Skills and Hobbies

Recognizing marketable skills and hobbies is essential for readers to discover lucrative and fulfilling side hustle opportunities. By identifying areas of expertise and interests that have commercial potential, individuals can leverage their talents

45

to create successful entrepreneurial ventures. Here's how the book guides readers through this process:

Reflect on Professional Experience:

Assess Professional Skills: Reflect on your professional experience and identify skills that are in demand in the marketplace. This may include expertise in areas such as project management, digital marketing, web development, content writing, graphic design, financial analysis, or consulting.

Evaluate Transferable Skills: Consider transferable skills that can be applied across different industries and roles, such as communication, problem-solving, leadership, time management, and teamwork.

Identify Specialized Knowledge: Identify specialized knowledge or certifications that you have acquired through formal education, training programs, or professional development courses.

Explore Creative Talents and Hobbies:

Identify Creative Abilities: Explore your creative talents and abilities, such as artistic skills, photography, writing, crafting, music, or culinary expertise. Consider how you can monetize these creative talents through avenues such as freelance work, online marketplaces, or creative workshops.

Assess Digital Skills: Evaluate your proficiency in digital skills and technologies, including social media management, graphic design software, video editing, website development, and e-commerce platforms. These digital skills can be

47

highly marketable in today's digital economy.

Consider Niche Interests: Reflect on niche interests and hobbies that have commercial potential. This may include niche markets such as sustainable living, fitness and wellness, pet care, outdoor activities, personal development, or specialized hobbies with dedicated communities and enthusiasts.

Research Market Demand and Trends:

Conduct Market Research: Research market demand and trends to identify areas of opportunity and potential gaps in the market. Look for emerging trends, consumer preferences, and niche markets that align with your skills and interests.

Explore Online Platforms: Explore online platforms, marketplaces, and communities related to your skills and hobbies. Pay attention to customer reviews, feedback, and discussions to gain insights into market demand and competition.

Identify Customer Pain Points: Identify customer pain points and challenges that your skills and expertise can address. Develop solutions and offerings that provide value to your target audience and differentiate you from competitors.

Test and Validate Ideas:

Test Minimum Viable Products (MVPs): Develop minimum viable products or prototypes to test the market demand for your offerings. Seek feedback from potential customers and iterate based on their input to refine your products or services.

Pilot Test Projects: Pilot test projects or services with a small

49

group of clients or customers to gauge interest and gather feedback. Use this feedback to make adjustments and improvements before scaling your offerings.

Monitor Performance Metrics: Monitor key performance metrics such as sales, customer acquisition costs, customer satisfaction, and retention rates to evaluate the success of your side hustle ventures. Adjust your strategies and offerings based on performance data to optimize results.

Understanding the Potential for Monetizing Skills and Interests

understanding the potential for monetizing skills and interests is crucial for readers to unlock opportunities for supplemental income and entrepreneurial success.

By recognizing the commercial value of their talents and passions, individuals can leverage them to create profitable side hustle ventures. Here's how the book guides readers through this process:

Identifying Marketable Skills and Talents

Self-Assessment: Encourage readers to conduct a thorough self-assessment to identify their skills, talents, and areas of expertise that have commercial potential. This includes evaluating professional skills, technical competencies, creative talents, and specialized knowledge.

Market Research: Guide readers to conduct market research to assess the demand for their skills and talents in the marketplace. This involves analyzing industry trends,

51

competitor offerings, customer preferences, and pricing strategies to identify opportunities for monetization.

Exploring Potential Revenue Streams:

Freelance Services: **Highlight the potential for offering freelance services based on readers' skills and expertise. This may include graphic design, writing, web development, digital marketing, consulting, photography, or tutoring services.**

Digital Products: **Introduce readers to the concept of creating and selling digital products such as e-books, online courses, templates, stock photography, music, or software applications. These digital products can be distributed through online platforms and marketplaces to reach a wider audience.**

Physical Products: Discuss the possibility of monetizing creative talents and hobbies by designing and selling physical products such as handmade crafts, artwork, clothing, accessories, or home decor items. Readers can explore e-commerce platforms, craft fairs, and artisan markets to showcase and sell their products.

Consulting and Coaching: Explore the potential for offering consulting or coaching services based on readers' expertise and industry knowledge. This may include business consulting, career coaching, life coaching, health coaching, or financial planning services.

Membership and Subscription Services: Introduce readers to the idea of creating membership sites or subscription services that offer exclusive content, resources, or community access to paying subscribers. This recurring revenue model can provide a steady income stream over time.

Developing a Monetization Strategy:

Define Target Audience: Encourage readers to define their target audience and understand their needs, preferences, and pain points. Tailor products and services to address specific customer challenges and provide value.

Pricing Strategy: Guide readers to develop a pricing strategy based on the perceived value of their offerings, market demand, competitor pricing, and cost considerations. Experiment with different pricing models and pricing tiers to find the optimal balance between affordability and profitability.

Marketing and Promotion: **Discuss strategies for marketing and promoting side hustle ventures to attract customers and drive sales. This may include social media marketing, content marketing, email marketing, influencer partnerships, search engine optimization (SEO), and paid advertising campaigns.**

Scaling and Growth Opportunities:

Encourage readers to explore opportunities for scaling and expanding their side hustle ventures over time. This may involve diversifying product offerings, expanding into new markets, forming strategic partnerships, or investing in marketing and infrastructure to support growth.

Emphasize the importance of tracking key performance indicators (KPIs) and metrics to measure the

55

success and performance of side hustle ventures. This includes monitoring sales, revenue, profit margins, customer acquisition costs, customer satisfaction, and retention rates.

CHAPTER 3

WEEKEND SIDE HUSTLE IDEAS

In "Weekend Side Hustle Techniques: After 5 to 9, How to Make Money on the Side in Your Spare Time," readers are presented with a variety of creative and practical side hustle ideas that they can explore to generate additional income and pursue their passions. Here are some weekend side hustle ideas highlighted in the book:

Freelance Writing or Editing:

Offer freelance writing services to businesses, bloggers, or online publications.

Provide editing and proofreading services for authors, students, or professionals.

Graphic Design Services:

Create logos, business cards, flyers, and other graphic design materials for small businesses and entrepreneurs.

Design digital graphics for websites, social media platforms, and marketing campaigns.

Photography Services:

Offer photography services for events, portraits, weddings, or family photoshoots.

Sell stock photos online to websites, bloggers, and content creators.

Online Tutoring or Teaching:

Provide online tutoring services in subjects such as math, science, language arts, or test preparation.

Create and sell online courses on platforms such as Udemy, Teachable, or Skillshare.

Virtual Assistant Services:

Offer virtual assistant services to entrepreneurs, small businesses, or busy professionals.

Assist with administrative tasks, email management, social media scheduling, and customer support.

Handmade Crafts and Artwork:

Create and sell handmade crafts such as jewelry, pottery, candles, or artwork on online marketplaces like Etsy or Shopify.

Participate in craft fairs, artisan markets, or local events to showcase and sell your creations.

Fitness Coaching or Personal Training:

Provide virtual or in-person fitness coaching and personal training sessions to individuals seeking to improve their health and fitness.

Develop personalized workout plans, provide nutritional guidance, and offer accountability and support to clients.

Pet Sitting or Dog Walking:

Offer pet sitting services for pet owners who need someone to care for their pets while they are away.

Provide dog walking services for busy professionals or individuals with busy schedules.

Consulting Services:

Offer consulting services in areas such as business development, marketing strategy, financial planning, or career coaching.

Share your expertise and knowledge to help clients solve problems, achieve goals, and improve their businesses or careers.

Airbnb Hosting or Vacation Rental Management:

List your property on Airbnb or other vacation rental platforms and earn income by hosting guests.

Provide vacation rental management services for property owners who need assistance with guest communication, cleaning, and maintenance.

Overview of Various Side Hustle Opportunities

readers are presented with a diverse range of side hustle opportunities designed to help them generate additional income, pursue their passions, and achieve greater financial independence. The book explores various avenues for leveraging spare time and skills to create profitable and fulfilling side hustle ventures. Here's an overview of the different side hustle opportunities highlighted in the book:

Freelance Services:

Writing and Editing: Offer freelance writing, editing, and proofreading services to businesses, bloggers, and authors.

Graphic Design: Provide graphic design services for businesses, startups, and individuals needing logos, branding materials, and marketing collateral.

Web Development: Create websites, landing pages, and online portfolios for clients in need of web development services.

Creative Endeavors:

Photography: Offer photography services for events, portraits, weddings, and commercial projects.

Handmade Crafts: Create and sell handmade crafts such as jewelry,

62

pottery, candles, and artwork through online platforms and local markets.

Music and Art: Monetize musical talents or artistic skills by offering music lessons, selling original artwork, or licensing creative content.

Online Business Ventures:

E-Commerce: Start an e-commerce store selling physical products, digital downloads, or print-on-demand merchandise.

Dropshipping: Launch a dropshipping business by sourcing products from suppliers and selling them to customers without holding inventory.

Affiliate Marketing: Partner with companies and promote their products or services through affiliate links to earn commissions on sales.

Consulting and Coaching:

Business Consulting: Offer consulting services in areas such as marketing, finance, human resources, and business development to help businesses improve performance and achieve growth.

Career Coaching: Provide career coaching and resume writing services to individuals seeking job search assistance and professional development.

Life Coaching: Offer life coaching services to help clients set and achieve personal goals, improve relationships, and enhance overall well-being.

Online Education and Training:

Online Tutoring: Provide online tutoring services in subjects such as math, science, languages, and test preparation to students of all ages.

Online Courses: Create and sell online courses on topics such as personal development, skills training, and specialized knowledge areas through platforms like Udemy, Teachable, and Skillshare.

Gig Economy Opportunities:

Ride-Sharing: Drive for ride-sharing services like Uber or Lyft to earn money transporting passengers in your spare time.

Delivery Services: Sign up as a delivery driver for food delivery platforms like DoorDash, Grubhub, or Postmates to deliver meals and groceries to customers.

Real Estate and Property Management:

Airbnb Hosting: Rent out spare rooms or properties on vacation rental platforms like Airbnb to earn income from short-term guests.

Property Management: Provide property management services for rental property owners, including tenant screening, leasing, maintenance, and rent collection.

Virtual Assistance and Administrative Support:

Virtual Assistant: Offer virtual assistant services to entrepreneurs, small businesses, and busy professionals to help with administrative tasks, email management, scheduling, and customer support.

Exploring Freelance Work and Gig Economy Platforms

Readers are introduced to the world of freelance work and gig economy platforms as viable avenues for generating additional income and pursuing flexible work opportunities. The book provides insights into how individuals can explore and navigate these platforms effectively. Here's an overview:

Understanding Freelance Work:

Definition: Freelance work involves providing services to clients on a project-by-project basis, typically as an independent contractor. Freelancers have the flexibility to choose their projects, set their rates, and work with multiple clients simultaneously.

Advantages: Freelance work offers flexibility, autonomy, and the opportunity to work on a variety of projects in different industries. Freelancers can control their schedules, choose projects that align with their skills and interests, and potentially earn higher rates compared to traditional employment.

Exploring Freelance Platforms:

Popular Platforms: Introduce readers to popular freelance platforms such as Upwork, Freelancer, Fiverr, Toptal, and Guru. These platforms connect freelancers with clients seeking a wide range of services, including writing, graphic design, programming, marketing, and more.

Creating Profiles: Guide readers through the process of creating compelling profiles on freelance platforms, highlighting their skills, expertise, and previous work experience. Emphasize the importance of crafting professional profiles that showcase their unique value proposition and attract potential clients.

Navigating Gig Economy Platforms:

Definition: Gig economy platforms connect independent workers with

68

short-term, on-demand work opportunities. These platforms offer a variety of services, including ride-sharing, food delivery, task completion, and more.

Examples: Highlight popular gig economy platforms such as Uber, Lyft, DoorDash, Instacart, TaskRabbit, and Postmates. Each platform caters to different types of services and allows individuals to earn money by completing tasks or providing services on a flexible basis.

Sign-Up Process: Walk readers through the sign-up process for gig economy platforms, which typically involves creating accounts, undergoing background checks, and meeting specific requirements depending on the type of service being offered.

Maximizing Opportunities:

Setting Rates: Help readers determine competitive rates for their services based on industry standards, skills, experience, and market demand. Encourage them to conduct research and adjust their rates accordingly to attract clients while ensuring fair compensation.

Building Reputation: Emphasize the importance of building a strong reputation and earning positive reviews on freelance and gig economy platforms. Satisfied clients and high ratings can significantly enhance credibility, attract more clients, and lead to repeat business.

Managing Time Effectively: Provide tips for managing time effectively and balancing freelance work with other commitments. Encourage readers to prioritize tasks, set boundaries, and establish realistic deadlines to maintain productivity and avoid burnout.

Leveraging Online Marketplaces for Selling Products or Services

Readers are introduced to the concept of leveraging online marketplaces as a strategic approach to selling products or services and generating additional income. The book explores the various opportunities and strategies available for individuals to establish a presence on online platforms and reach a wider audience. Here's an overview:

Understanding Online Marketplaces:

Definition: Online marketplaces are digital platforms that connect buyers and sellers, facilitating transactions for a wide range of products and services. These platforms provide a centralized space for businesses and individuals to showcase their offerings, reach potential customers, and complete transactions securely.

Examples: Introduce readers to popular online marketplaces such as Amazon, eBay, Etsy, Shopify, and Alibaba. Each platform caters to different types of products and services, ranging from physical goods to digital downloads and creative handmade items.

Selling Physical Products:

Product Selection: Guide readers in selecting or creating products that align with market demand, trends, and customer preferences. Encourage them to consider factors such as product quality, uniqueness, and competitive pricing.

Listing Optimization: Provide tips for optimizing product listings on online marketplaces to improve visibility and attract potential buyers. This includes writing compelling product descriptions, using high-quality images, and incorporating relevant keywords for search engine optimization (SEO).

Fulfillment Options: Discuss fulfillment options such as self-fulfillment, third-party logistics (3PL) services, and fulfillment by Amazon (FBA). Help readers evaluate the pros and cons of each option based on factors like cost, scalability, and operational efficiency.

Offering Digital Products and Services:

Digital Downloads: Explore the opportunity to sell digital products such as e-books, courses, templates, software, and digital artwork. Discuss platforms like Gumroad, Teachable, and Payhip that enable creators to sell and deliver digital downloads directly to customers.

Online Services: Highlight the potential for offering online services such as consulting, coaching, tutoring, graphic design, writing, and virtual assistance. Emphasize the importance of clearly defining service offerings, setting pricing structures, and showcasing expertise and credentials to attract clients.

Building Brand Awareness and Trust:

Branding: Stress the importance of building a strong brand identity and reputation on online marketplaces. Encourage readers to develop cohesive branding elements such as logos, packaging, and messaging that resonate with their target audience.

Customer Reviews: **Emphasize the role of customer reviews and testimonials in building trust and credibility with potential buyers. Encourage readers to prioritize customer satisfaction, address feedback promptly, and maintain transparency and integrity in their interactions.**

Marketing and Promotion:

Social Media Marketing: Discuss strategies for leveraging social media platforms such as Instagram, Facebook, Twitter, and Pinterest to promote products and services, engage with customers, and drive traffic to online marketplace listings.

Paid Advertising: **Introduce readers to paid advertising options such as sponsored product listings, pay-per-click (PPC) ads, and display advertising on online marketplaces and external platforms. Help them** develop targeted advertising campaigns to reach their desired audience effectively.

Exploring Offline Opportunities and Local Markets

Readers are encouraged to explore offline opportunities and tap into local markets as viable avenues for generating income and pursuing entrepreneurial ventures. The book emphasizes the potential of offline channels and local communities for launching successful side hustles. Here's an overview:

Identifying Offline Opportunities: Definition: Offline opportunities refer to business ventures and income-generating activities that occur outside the realm of digital platforms and online channels. These opportunities often involve direct interaction with customers and participation in local events, markets, and communities.

Examples: Offline opportunities encompass a wide range of activities, including selling products at local markets, offering services in-person, participating in community events, and leveraging traditional marketing channels such as print media, flyers, and word-of-mouth referrals.

Exploring Local Markets:

Farmers Markets: Farmers markets provide a platform for local artisans, farmers, and entrepreneurs to showcase and sell their products directly to consumers. Readers can explore opportunities to participate as vendors and sell handmade crafts, artisanal goods, baked goods, and locally sourced produce.

77

Flea Markets and Craft Fairs: **Flea markets and craft fairs attract shoppers seeking unique and handcrafted items. Individuals can rent booth space at these events to sell handmade crafts, vintage goods, collectibles, and other niche products.**

Pop-Up Shops: **Pop-up shops offer temporary retail spaces where entrepreneurs can showcase and sell their products for a limited time. Readers can explore opportunities to collaborate with local businesses or rent vacant storefronts to host pop-up shops in high-traffic areas.**

Offering In-Person Services:

Workshops and Classes: **Readers can leverage their skills and expertise to offer in-person workshops, classes, and training sessions in their local communities. Topics may include cooking classes, art workshops,** fitness sessions, DIY projects, and educational seminars.

Home Services: Individuals with specialized skills or trades can offer home services such as landscaping, house cleaning, home repair, painting, and interior decorating to local homeowners and businesses.

Event Services: Entrepreneurs can provide event services such as event planning, catering, photography, entertainment, and venue rental for weddings, parties, corporate events, and community gatherings.

Leveraging Traditional Marketing Channels:

Local Advertising: Encourage readers to explore traditional advertising channels such as newspapers, magazines, radio, and local television stations to promote their

79

side hustle ventures and reach local audiences.

Flyers and Direct Mail: Distributing flyers, postcards, and direct mailers in targeted neighborhoods and communities can help raise awareness of products, services, and upcoming events.

Networking and Referrals: Building relationships with local businesses, organizations, and community leaders can lead to valuable networking opportunities and word-of-mouth referrals for side hustle ventures.

Evaluating the Feasibility and Profitability of Different Ideas

Readers are guided through a systematic process of evaluating the feasibility and profitability of different side hustle ideas. This critical step helps individuals make informed decisions about which ventures to pursue based on their resources, skills, interests, and market opportunities. Here's how the book approaches this evaluation process:

Define Success Criteria:

Begin by defining clear criteria for success based on personal goals, financial objectives, and lifestyle preferences. Consider factors such as desired income level, time commitment, work-life balance, and long-term sustainability.

Conduct Market Research:

Research the market landscape to assess demand, competition, and trends related to each side hustle idea. Identify target audiences, understand their needs and preferences, and evaluate the viability of the market opportunity.

Analyze industry reports, competitor offerings, customer reviews, and consumer behavior to gather insights and validate assumptions about market dynamics.

Evaluate Profitability:

Estimate the potential revenue and costs associated with each side hustle idea to determine its profitability. Consider factors such as pricing strategies, sales volume projections, production costs, overhead expenses, and profit margins.

Calculate key financial metrics such as return on investment (ROI), break-even point, gross profit, and net profit to assess the financial viability of each idea.

Assess Resource Requirements:

Identify the resources and investments required to launch and operate each side hustle idea effectively. This may include financial capital, time commitments, equipment, supplies, technology, skills, and human resources.

Evaluate the availability of resources and assess whether you have the necessary capabilities and capacity to execute the idea successfully.

Consider Risks and Challenges: Anticipate potential risks, challenges, and obstacles that may arise during the execution of each side hustle idea. Assess factors such as market volatility, regulatory compliance, supply chain disruptions, competitive threats, and changing consumer preferences.

Develop contingency plans and mitigation strategies to address risks and minimize negative impacts on the business.

Conduct Pilot Tests and Experiments:

Consider conducting pilot tests or experiments to validate assumptions, test market response, and gather feedback from potential customers. Launch small-scale versions of the side hustle idea to assess feasibility and refine the business model based on real-world insights.

Monitor key performance indicators (KPIs) and metrics to track progress, measure success, and identify areas for improvement.

Make Informed Decisions:

Based on the findings from market research, financial analysis, resource assessment, and risk evaluation, make informed decisions about which side hustle ideas to pursue. Prioritize ideas that align with your

strengths, interests, and long-term goals.

CHAPTER 4

TIME MANAGEMENT STRATEGIES

Effective time management is emphasized as a key factor in balancing side hustle endeavors with other commitments and responsibilities. The book offers practical strategies to help readers optimize their time and maximize productivity during their spare time. Here are some time management strategies highlighted in the book:

Prioritize Tasks:

Identify and prioritize tasks based on their importance and urgency. Focus on high-priority activities that align with your goals and contribute to the success of your side hustle ventures.

Use techniques such as the Eisenhower Matrix or ABC prioritization to categorize tasks and allocate time and resources accordingly.

Set Clear Goals:

Define clear and specific goals for your side hustle ventures, including short-term objectives and long-term milestones. Break down larger goals into smaller, manageable tasks to maintain focus and motivation.

Regularly review and revise your goals to adapt to changing circumstances and priorities.

Create a Schedule:

Establish a structured schedule or routine for your spare time activities, including dedicated time blocks for side hustle work, personal activities, and relaxation. Set specific start and end times for each task to maintain discipline and accountability.

Use digital tools such as calendar apps, task managers, and productivity apps to organize your schedule and set reminders for important deadlines and appointments.

Batch Similar Tasks:

Group similar tasks together and tackle them in batches to minimize context switching and maximize efficiency. For example, dedicate specific time blocks for content creation, client communication, administrative tasks, and marketing efforts.

Prioritize tasks that require similar levels of focus and concentration during peak productivity hours.

Practice Time Blocking:

Implement time blocking techniques to allocate dedicated time slots for specific activities and minimize distractions. Reserve uninterrupted blocks of time for focused work on your side hustle projects, free from distractions and interruptions.

Communicate your availability and boundaries to family members, friends, and colleagues to minimize disruptions during focused work sessions.

Delegate and Outsource:

Identify tasks that can be delegated or outsourced to others to free up your time and focus on high-value activities. Consider hiring virtual assistants, freelancers, or subcontractors to handle repetitive tasks, administrative work, or specialized projects.

Clearly define expectations, provide clear instructions, and establish communication channels to ensure effective collaboration and delegation.

Practice Self-Care:

Prioritize self-care and well-being to maintain physical and mental health while juggling multiple responsibilities. Schedule regular breaks, exercise, and relaxation activities to recharge and rejuvenate.

Listen to your body and mind, and be mindful of signs of burnout or overwhelm. Practice stress management techniques such as mindfulness, meditation, and deep breathing exercises to reduce stress and enhance resilience.

Balancing Full-Time Commitments with Side Hustle Endeavors

Readers are provided with strategies and insights on how to effectively balance full-time commitments with their side hustle endeavors. Recognizing the demands of a full-time job alongside the pursuit of entrepreneurial ventures, the book offers practical advice to help individuals manage their time, energy, and priorities effectively. Here are key considerations and strategies highlighted in the book:

Define Priorities:

Clearly define your priorities and objectives for both your full-time job and your side hustle endeavors. Determine what is most important to you in terms of career advancement, financial goals, personal fulfillment, and work-life balance.

91

Time Management:

Utilize effective time management techniques to allocate dedicated time slots for your full-time job, side hustle projects, personal activities, and relaxation. Establish a structured schedule that allows you to balance your various commitments without feeling overwhelmed.

Prioritize tasks based on their importance and urgency, and use tools such as calendars, planners, and task lists to stay organized and on track.

Set Boundaries:

Establish clear boundaries between your full-time job and your side hustle activities to prevent burnout and maintain boundaries between work and personal life. Communicate your availability and limitations to colleagues, clients, and stakeholders to manage expectations effectively.

Respect your personal time and avoid allowing side hustle activities to encroach on your rest and relaxation time, as this can lead to increased stress and fatigue.

Optimize Productivity:

Identify peak productivity periods during the day and allocate these times to focus on high-priority tasks and projects. Minimize distractions and interruptions during focused work sessions to maximize productivity and efficiency.

Break larger tasks into smaller, manageable steps to avoid feeling overwhelmed and maintain momentum in your side hustle endeavors.

Delegate and Outsource:

Delegate tasks and responsibilities within both your full-time job and your side hustle ventures to alleviate workload pressures and leverage the expertise of others. Consider outsourcing tasks such as administrative work, project management, and specialized services to freelancers or virtual assistants.

Clearly communicate expectations, provide adequate training and support, and establish effective communication channels to ensure smooth collaboration and delegation.

Practice Self-Care:

Prioritize self-care and well-being to maintain physical and mental health while juggling multiple commitments. Make time for activities that recharge and rejuvenate you, such as exercise, hobbies, socializing, and relaxation.

Listen to your body and mind, and be mindful of signs of stress, fatigue, and burnout. Practice stress management techniques such as mindfulness, meditation, and deep breathing exercises to reduce stress and enhance resilience.

Evaluate and Adjust:

Regularly evaluate your workload, commitments, and priorities to ensure alignment with your overarching goals and objectives. Be open to adjusting your strategies and approaches as needed to accommodate changing circumstances and evolving priorities.

Seek feedback from trusted mentors, peers, or advisors to gain perspective and insights on how to optimize your balancing act between full-time commitments and side hustle endeavors.

Creating a Structured Schedule for Side Hustle Activities

Readers are guided through the process of creating a structured schedule that allows for effective time management and productivity in their side hustle activities. Recognizing the importance of balancing various commitments and responsibilities, the book offers practical advice on how to allocate time efficiently and optimize productivity. Here's how to create a structured schedule for side hustle activities:

Assess Available Time:

Begin by assessing your available time outside of your primary commitments, such as your full-time job, family obligations, and personal activities. Identify pockets of time during evenings, weekends, or other free periods when you can dedicate focused attention to your side hustle endeavors.

Define Goals and Priorities:

Clearly define your goals and priorities for your side hustle activities. Determine what you hope to achieve, whether it's generating additional income, pursuing a passion project, or developing new skills. Break down larger goals into smaller, actionable steps that can be integrated into your schedule.

Allocate Dedicated Time Blocks:

Allocate dedicated time blocks in your schedule specifically for your side hustle activities. Consider scheduling consistent blocks of time each day or week to work on different aspects of your side hustle, such as product development, marketing, client meetings, or administrative tasks.

Be intentional about how you allocate your time, and prioritize tasks based on their importance and urgency. Set specific start and end times for each time block to maintain discipline and accountability.

Establish a Routine:

Establish a consistent routine for your side hustle activities to create structure and rhythm in your schedule. Determine the best times of day for you to focus on different types of tasks, taking into account your energy levels and productivity patterns.

Incorporate rituals and habits into your routine to signal the start and end of side hustle work sessions. This could include setting up a dedicated workspace, brewing a cup of coffee, or reviewing your task list before diving into work.

Use Time Management Tools:

Leverage time management tools and techniques to organize your schedule and stay on track with your side hustle activities. Consider using digital tools such as calendar apps, task managers, and productivity apps to schedule tasks, set reminders, and track progress.

Experiment with different methods of time blocking, prioritization, and task management to find what works best for you. Regularly review and adjust your schedule as needed to accommodate changes in priorities or workload.

Plan for Flexibility:

Recognize that unexpected events and disruptions may occur that require flexibility in your schedule.

99

Build in buffer time and allow for adjustments to accommodate shifting priorities or unforeseen circumstances.

Practice resilience and adaptability in managing your schedule, and maintain a positive mindset when faced with challenges or setbacks. Embrace opportunities for learning and growth, and view changes in your schedule as opportunities to refine your approach.

Maintain Work-Life Balance:

Prioritize work-life balance and avoid overcommitting yourself to your side hustle activities at the expense of your well-being and personal life. Set boundaries around your side hustle work hours and make time for rest, relaxation, and leisure activities.

Regularly evaluate your schedule to ensure that you're allocating sufficient time for self-care,

100

relationships, and other aspects of your life that contribute to overall happiness and fulfillment.

Prioritizing Tasks and Maximizing Productivity During Spare Time

Readers are guided through strategies to prioritize tasks and maximize productivity during their spare time, allowing them to make significant progress in their side hustle endeavors. Recognizing the limited nature of spare time and the importance of using it effectively, the book offers practical advice on how to identify key tasks and optimize productivity. Here's how to prioritize tasks and maximize productivity during spare time:

Identify High-Priority Tasks:
Begin by identifying high-priority tasks that are critical to the success

and progress of your side hustle endeavors. These tasks may include revenue-generating activities, client deliverables, marketing efforts, or strategic planning initiatives.

Focus on tasks that have the greatest impact on moving your side hustle forward and achieving your long-term goals. Consider the urgency and importance of each task when prioritizing your to-do list.

Use the Eisenhower Matrix:

Apply the Eisenhower Matrix, a productivity tool that helps categorize tasks based on their urgency and importance. Divide tasks into four quadrants: urgent and important, important but not urgent, urgent but not important, and neither urgent nor important.

Prioritize tasks in the first quadrant (urgent and important) as top priorities, followed by tasks in the

102

second quadrant (important but not urgent). Delegate or eliminate tasks in the third and fourth quadrants as appropriate.

Set SMART Goals:

Set SMART goals for your side hustle activities: Specific, Measurable, Achievable, Relevant, and Time-bound. Break down larger goals into smaller, actionable steps that can be completed during your spare time.

Ensure that your goals are clear, quantifiable, and aligned with your overall vision for your side hustle. Track your progress toward achieving these goals and adjust your priorities as needed.

Establish Daily and Weekly Priorities:

Establish daily and weekly priorities for your spare time activities, based on the tasks and goals you've identified. Create a list of tasks to be completed each day, focusing on the most important and time-sensitive items first.

Allocate specific time blocks in your schedule for working on these priorities, ensuring that you dedicate focused attention and energy to completing them effectively.

Leverage Time Blocking:

Implement time blocking techniques to allocate dedicated time slots for different activities and tasks. Schedule specific blocks of time for working on your side hustle projects, responding to emails, conducting research, or engaging in marketing efforts.

Limit distractions and interruptions during these focused work sessions by setting boundaries and creating a conducive work environment. Use techniques such as the Pomodoro

Technique to break work periods into smaller intervals with regular breaks.

Practice the Two-Minute Rule:

Embrace the Two-Minute Rule, which states that if a task can be completed in two minutes or less, it should be done immediately. Tackle small, low-effort tasks during spare moments to prevent them from accumulating and becoming overwhelming.

By addressing quick tasks promptly, you can maintain momentum and prevent them from becoming distractions or sources of procrastination.

Reflect and Iterate:

Regularly reflect on your productivity habits and identify areas for improvement in how you prioritize tasks and manage your spare time. Experiment with different techniques and strategies to find what works best for you.

Be open to feedback and insights from your own experiences and those of others. Continuously iterate and refine your approach to productivity to enhance effectiveness and efficiency over time.

By prioritizing tasks and maximizing productivity during spare time, readers of "Weekend Side Hustle Techniques" can make significant strides in advancing their side hustle endeavors and achieving their entrepreneurial goals. By adopting effective strategies and habits, individuals can optimize their use of spare time and unlock their full potential in pursuit of their passions and aspirations.

CHAPTER 5

FINANCIAL PLANNING AND INVESTMENT

Readers are introduced to the importance of financial planning and investment as integral components of building wealth and achieving long-term financial stability through side hustle endeavors. The book emphasizes the significance of sound financial management practices and strategic investment decisions to maximize the returns from spare time activities. Here's how financial planning and investment are addressed in the book:

Setting Financial Goals:

Begin by setting clear and achievable financial goals for your side hustle ventures. Define short-term and long-term objectives, such as earning a specific amount of additional income per month, paying off debt, saving for a major purchase, or investing for retirement.

Ensure that your financial goals are realistic, measurable, and aligned with your overall financial priorities and aspirations.

Budgeting and Expense Management:

Implement effective budgeting and expense management practices to track your income and expenses related to your side hustle activities. Create a detailed budget that outlines your projected earnings, fixed expenses, variable costs, and savings goals.

Monitor your spending habits and identify areas where you can reduce unnecessary expenses and optimize your cash flow. Allocate a portion of your side hustle income towards savings, emergency funds, debt repayment, and investment opportunities.

Diversification of Income Streams:

Recognize the importance of diversifying your sources of income to minimize risk

Setting Financial Goals for Side Hustle Income

Readers are encouraged to set clear and achievable financial goals to guide their side hustle endeavors and maximize the impact of their spare time activities. Setting financial goals provides direction, motivation, and a roadmap for effectively managing side hustle income and achieving desired financial outcomes. Here's how to set financial goals for side hustle income:

Define Specific Objectives:

Begin by defining specific financial objectives that you aim to achieve through your side hustle income. These objectives may include:

Earning a certain amount of additional income per month or year.

Paying off existing debt, such as credit card balances, student loans, or car loans.

Saving for short-term goals, such as a vacation, home renovation, or major purchase.

Building an emergency fund to cover unexpected expenses or financial setbacks.

Investing for long-term goals, such as retirement savings, education funds, or wealth accumulation.

Make Goals Measurable:

Ensure that your financial goals are measurable and quantifiable, allowing you to track progress and assess success over time. Use specific metrics, such as dollar amounts or percentages, to define the achievement criteria for each goal.

Break down larger goals into smaller, incremental milestones that are easier to monitor and achieve. Celebrate small victories along the way to maintain motivation and momentum.

Align Goals with Personal Values:

Align your financial goals with your personal values, priorities, and aspirations. Consider what matters most to you in terms of financial security, freedom, lifestyle preferences, and long-term well-being.

Reflect on your values and goals to ensure that your side hustle activities are in harmony with your overall vision for your life and future financial success.

Set Realistic and Achievable Targets:

Set realistic and achievable targets for your side hustle income based on your current financial situation, skills, resources, and time constraints. Avoid setting overly ambitious goals that may be difficult to attain within a reasonable timeframe.

Take into account factors such as market conditions, demand for your products or services, competition, and seasonality when setting income targets for your side hustle.

112

Establish Timeframes and Deadlines:

Establish clear timeframes and deadlines for achieving your financial goals, providing a sense of urgency and accountability to your actions. Define specific deadlines for reaching each milestone or target within your overall financial plan.

Consider short-term, medium-term, and long-term timeframes for your financial goals, allowing for a balanced approach to goal-setting and progress tracking.

Create an Action Plan:

Develop a detailed action plan outlining the steps and strategies you will implement to achieve your financial goals. Break down each goal into actionable tasks, identifying the resources, skills, and support needed to execute your plan effectively.

113

Prioritize tasks based on their importance and urgency, allocating time and resources accordingly to maximize efficiency and productivity.

Monitor Progress and Adjust as Needed:

Regularly monitor your progress toward achieving your financial goals, tracking income, expenses, savings, and investment performance. Review your financial statements, budget reports, and savings accounts on a monthly or quarterly basis.

Be proactive in identifying areas where adjustments may be needed to stay on track with your goals. Evaluate the effectiveness of your strategies and make necessary modifications to overcome obstacles or capitalize on opportunities.

Budgeting and Managing Expenses Effectively

Readers are introduced to the importance of budgeting and managing expenses effectively to optimize their financial resources and achieve their side hustle goals. By implementing sound financial management practices, individuals can make the most of their spare time income and build a solid foundation for financial stability and success. Here's how budgeting and expense management are addressed in the book:

Establish a Budget:

Begin by creating a comprehensive budget that outlines your income, expenses, savings goals, and financial priorities. Take into account all sources of income, including earnings from your full-time job and additional income generated through side hustle activities.

Categorize your expenses into fixed expenses (e.g., rent or mortgage, utilities, insurance premiums) and variable expenses (e.g., groceries, entertainment, discretionary spending). Allocate funds to each expense category based on your financial needs and priorities.

Track Income and Expenses:

Track your income and expenses regularly to monitor cash flow and ensure that you're staying within your budgetary limits. Use tools such as spreadsheets, budgeting apps, or financial management software to record transactions, categorize expenses, and analyze spending patterns.

Review your financial statements, bank accounts, and credit card statements on a monthly basis to identify any discrepancies, overspending, or areas where adjustments may be needed.

Identify Opportunities for Savings:

Identify opportunities for reducing expenses and saving money without compromising your quality of life or essential needs. Look for areas where you can cut back on discretionary spending, negotiate better deals or discounts, or eliminate unnecessary expenses altogether.

Consider adopting cost-saving strategies such as meal planning, shopping in bulk, using coupons or promotional codes, and exploring alternative transportation options to reduce commuting costs.

Prioritize Financial Goals:

Prioritize your financial goals and allocate resources accordingly to ensure that you're making progress toward achieving your objectives. Identify short-term goals (e.g., building an emergency fund, paying off debt), medium-term goals (e.g., saving for a vacation or home renovation), and long-term goals (e.g., retirement savings, investment goals).

Allocate a portion of your side hustle income toward each of your financial goals, taking into account the time horizon, urgency, and importance of each objective.

Build an Emergency Fund:

Establish an emergency fund to cover unexpected expenses or financial emergencies that may arise. Aim to set aside three to six months' worth of living expenses in a

118

separate savings account or liquid investment vehicle.

Contribute to your emergency fund regularly, even if it means starting with small amounts and gradually increasing your contributions over time. Having a financial safety net provides peace of mind and protects against unforeseen circumstances.

Avoid Debt and Manage Credit Wisely:

Avoid accumulating high-interest debt whenever possible and manage existing debt responsibly. Pay off credit card balances in full each month to avoid interest charges and minimize debt accumulation.

Use credit cards and other forms of credit judiciously, and be mindful of interest rates, fees, and repayment terms. Monitor your credit score regularly and take steps to improve or maintain a healthy credit profile.

Review and Adjust Regularly: Review your budget and expense management practices regularly to ensure that they remain aligned with your financial goals and priorities. Make adjustments as needed to accommodate changes in income, expenses, or financial circumstances.

Stay flexible and adaptable in your approach to budgeting and expense management, and be open to exploring new strategies or opportunities for optimizing your financial resources.

Investing Profits for Long-Term Financial Stability

In "Weekend Side Hustle Techniques: After 5 to 9, How to Make Money on the Side in Your Spare Time," readers are enlightened about the importance of investing profits generated from side hustle endeavors to secure long-term financial stability and build wealth. The book emphasizes the significance of strategic investment decisions in leveraging spare time income to achieve financial independence and future prosperity. Here's how investing profits for long-term financial stability is addressed in the book:

Understand Investment Principles:

Educate yourself about fundamental investment principles, including risk and return, diversification, asset allocation, and investment vehicles. Gain insights into different investment options and strategies available for growing wealth over time.

Set Investment Goals:

Define clear and measurable investment goals aligned with your long-term financial objectives. Consider factors such as retirement planning, wealth accumulation, education funding, and legacy planning when setting investment goals for your side hustle profits.

Determine Risk Tolerance:

Assess your risk tolerance and investment preferences to determine the most suitable investment approach for your financial situation and temperament. Consider factors such as age, investment horizon, financial goals, and comfort level with market fluctuations.

Explore Investment Options:

Explore a diverse range of investment options available for deploying your side hustle profits, including stocks, bonds, mutual funds, exchange-traded funds (ETFs), real estate, retirement accounts, and alternative investments.

Conduct thorough research and due diligence on potential investment opportunities, evaluating factors such as historical performance, risk profile, fees, liquidity, and tax implications.

Build a Balanced Portfolio:

Construct a well-diversified investment portfolio tailored to your financial goals, risk tolerance, and time horizon. Allocate assets across different asset classes, sectors, and geographical regions to minimize risk and maximize potential returns.

Consider adopting a strategic asset allocation strategy that aligns with your investment objectives and adjusts over time based on changing market conditions and personal circumstances.

Invest Regularly and Consistently:

Implement a disciplined investment approach by investing profits from your side hustle endeavors regularly and consistently over time. Embrace the power of compounding returns by reinvesting dividends, interest, and capital gains to accelerate wealth accumulation.

Set up automated contributions to investment accounts or retirement plans to ensure consistent funding and avoid market timing pitfalls.

Monitor and Rebalance:

Monitor the performance of your investment portfolio regularly and rebalance as needed to maintain alignment with your target asset allocation and risk tolerance. Review your portfolio holdings, asset allocation, and investment objectives on a periodic basis.

Stay informed about market trends, economic indicators, and geopolitical developments that may impact your investment decisions. Be prepared to make adjustments to your portfolio based on changing market dynamics and emerging opportunities or risks.

Seek Professional Guidance:

Consider seeking professional guidance from financial advisors, investment professionals, or wealth managers to develop a personalized investment strategy and optimize your portfolio for long-term growth and stability.

Leverage the expertise and insights of investment professionals to navigate complex financial markets, optimize tax efficiency, and mitigate investment risks effectively.

By investing profits from side hustle activities for long-term financial stability, readers of "Weekend Side Hustle Techniques" can harness the power of compound interest and strategic asset allocation to build wealth and achieve their financial goals over time. With patience, discipline, and informed decision-making, individuals can secure a brighter financial future and enjoy the fruits of their labor from their spare time endeavors.

CHAPTER 6

MARKETING AND PROMOTION

Readers are provided with valuable insights and strategies on marketing and promotion to effectively promote their side hustle endeavors and attract customers. Recognizing the importance of visibility and brand awareness in driving business success, the book offers practical advice on how to develop and implement marketing strategies tailored to the unique needs and objectives of side hustle ventures. Here's how marketing and promotion are addressed in the book:

Define Your Target Audience:

Begin by identifying and understanding your target audience the specific demographic or niche market that your products or services cater to. Conduct market research to gain insights into their preferences, needs, behaviors, and purchasing habits.

Segment your target audience based on factors such as age, gender, location, income level, interests, and pain points to tailor your marketing efforts more effectively.

Develop a Compelling Value Proposition:

Clearly articulate your value proposition the unique benefits and value that your products or services offer to customers. Differentiate your side hustle from competitors by highlighting its unique selling points, features, and advantages.

Communicate your value proposition effectively through your marketing materials, messaging, and brand positioning to resonate with your target audience and compel them to take action.

Establish a Strong Brand Identity:

Build a strong and memorable brand identity that reflects your side hustle's values, personality, and story. Develop cohesive branding elements, such as a logo, color palette, typography, and visual imagery, that convey your brand's identity and evoke emotional connections with customers.

Consistently apply your brand identity across all marketing channels and touchpoints to reinforce brand recognition and foster brand loyalty among customers.

Leverage Digital Marketing Channels:

Embrace digital marketing channels and platforms to reach and engage with your target audience online. Explore a diverse range of digital marketing tactics, including:

Content marketing: Create valuable, informative, and engaging content that educates and entertains your audience while showcasing your expertise and offerings.

Social media marketing: Establish a strong presence on social media platforms relevant to your target audience. Share compelling content, engage with followers, and leverage paid advertising to expand your reach and drive traffic to your side hustle.

Email marketing: Build an email list of subscribers interested in your products or services. Send personalized, targeted email campaigns to nurture leads, promote special offers, and encourage repeat purchases.

Search engine optimization (SEO): Optimize your website and online content to improve visibility and ranking in search engine results. Use relevant keywords, meta tags, and backlinks to enhance your site's search engine optimization and attract organic traffic.

Network and Collaborate:

Leverage your personal and professional networks to expand your reach and connect with potential customers, partners, and collaborators. Attend networking events, industry conferences, and community gatherings to build relationships and foster mutually beneficial partnerships.

Collaborate with complementary businesses, influencers, bloggers, and content creators to amplify your marketing efforts and reach new audiences. Explore opportunities for cross-promotion, guest blogging, joint ventures, and affiliate partnerships to leverage shared audiences and resources.

Monitor and Measure Performance:

Monitor the performance of your marketing campaigns and initiatives using key performance indicators (KPIs) and analytics tools. Track metrics such as website traffic, social media engagement, email open rates, conversion rates, and return on investment (ROI).

Analyze the data collected to gain insights into what's working well and where there's room for improvement. Adjust your marketing strategies and tactics based on performance data to optimize results and maximize impact.

Iterate and Adapt:

Be flexible and adaptable in your approach to marketing and promotion, and be willing to experiment with new ideas, tactics, and channels. Stay attuned to changes in consumer preferences, industry trends, and competitive landscape to remain relevant and responsive.

Continuously iterate and refine your marketing strategies based on feedback, insights, and evolving market dynamics. Embrace a mindset of continuous improvement and innovation to stay ahead of the curve and drive sustainable growth for your side hustle.

133

Building a Personal Brand for Side Hustle Ventures

Readers are introduced to the concept of building a personal brand as a foundational strategy for success in their side hustle endeavors. A personal brand encompasses the unique identity, values, expertise, and reputation that individuals cultivate to distinguish themselves and their offerings in the marketplace. Here's how building a personal brand is addressed in the book:

Define Your Unique Value Proposition:

Begin by defining your unique value proposition the qualities, skills, and attributes that set you apart from others in your niche or industry. Consider what makes you distinctive, memorable, and valuable to your target audience.

Identify your strengths, passions, and areas of expertise that you can leverage to build credibility and authority in your chosen field or market.

Clarify Your Brand Identity:

Clarify your brand identity by articulating your mission, vision, and values as they relate to your side hustle ventures. Consider the overarching purpose and impact you aim to achieve through your products, services, or contributions.

Develop a cohesive brand identity that reflects your personality, style, and values across all aspects of your side hustle activities, including your logo, website, social media profiles, packaging, and marketing materials.

Establish Your Online Presence:

Establish a strong online presence to amplify your personal brand and reach a broader audience of potential customers or clients. Create professional profiles on relevant social media platforms, such as LinkedIn, Instagram, Facebook, and Twitter.

Curate compelling content that showcases your expertise, insights, and personality to engage and attract followers. Share valuable information, insights, and resources that resonate with your target audience and demonstrate your thought leadership.

Cultivate Thought Leadership:

Position yourself as a thought leader and subject matter expert within your niche or industry by sharing your knowledge, experiences, and perspectives through blog posts, articles, podcasts, videos, webinars, and speaking engagements.

Offer unique insights, practical tips, and actionable advice that address the needs, challenges, and aspirations of your target audience. Consistently deliver high-quality content that educates, inspires, and empowers your followers.

Engage with Your Audience:

Foster meaningful connections and interactions with your audience by actively engaging with them on social media, forums, groups, and community platforms. Respond promptly to comments, messages, and inquiries to demonstrate your accessibility and responsiveness.

Encourage dialogue, feedback, and participation by asking questions, soliciting opinions, and inviting contributions from your audience. Create opportunities for two-way communication and collaboration to build trust and rapport with your community.

Deliver Exceptional Value:

Prioritize delivering exceptional value and exceptional customer experiences in every interaction with your audience, customers, or clients. Strive to exceed expectations and consistently deliver products, services, or solutions that solve real problems and fulfill genuine needs.

Focus on building long-term relationships and loyalty with your customers by demonstrating integrity, reliability, and authenticity in your actions and communications.

Evolve and Adapt:

Continuously evolve and adapt your personal brand strategy in response to changing market dynamics, emerging trends, and feedback from your audience. Stay agile and open-minded to new opportunities for growth and innovation.

Regularly assess your brand performance, monitor key metrics and indicators, and seek opportunities for optimization and enhancement. Embrace experimentation and iteration as essential components of the branding process.

Utilizing Social Media and Online Marketing Channels

Readers are introduced to the significance of leveraging social media and online marketing channels as essential components of their side hustle strategies. By effectively utilizing digital platforms, individuals can expand their reach, engage with their target audience, and promote their products or services to drive growth and success in their spare time endeavors. Here's how utilizing

139

social media and online marketing channels is addressed in the book:

Establish a Strong Online Presence:

Begin by establishing a strong online presence across relevant social media platforms and online marketing channels that resonate with your target audience. Identify platforms where your potential customers or clients are most active and engaged.

Create professional profiles and pages for your side hustle venture on platforms such as Facebook, Instagram, Twitter, LinkedIn, Pinterest, and TikTok, depending on your target market and business objectives.

Define Your Audience and Objectives:

Define your target audience and marketing objectives to guide your social media and online marketing efforts effectively. Understand the demographics, interests, behaviors, and preferences of your ideal customers or clients.

Clarify your marketing goals, whether they involve increasing brand awareness, driving website traffic, generating leads, increasing sales, or fostering customer engagement and loyalty.

Craft Compelling Content:

Craft compelling and relevant content that resonates with your target audience and aligns with your brand identity and messaging. Create a content calendar to plan and schedule your posts, ensuring consistency and frequency in your communication.

Experiment with different content formats, such as text posts, images, videos, infographics, polls, quizzes, and stories, to capture attention and stimulate engagement on social media platforms.

Engage and Interact with Your Audience:

Foster meaningful engagement and interaction with your audience by responding promptly to comments, messages, and inquiries. Encourage dialogue, feedback, and user-generated content to foster a sense of community and connection.

Host live Q&A sessions, webinars, virtual events, and contests to actively engage with your audience and provide value-added experiences that differentiate your brand and build loyalty.

Implement Targeted Advertising Campaigns:

Utilize targeted advertising campaigns on social media platforms to reach specific segments of your target audience and amplify your brand message. Leverage advanced targeting options based on demographics, interests, behaviors, and custom audience segments.

Experiment with different ad formats, objectives, and creative elements to optimize campaign performance and maximize return on investment (ROI) for your advertising spend.

Monitor Performance and Analytics:

Monitor the performance of your social media and online marketing campaigns using analytics tools and platform insights. Track key metrics such as reach, engagement, clicks, conversions, and return on ad spend (ROAS) to measure the effectiveness of your efforts.

Analyze data trends, patterns, and audience feedback to gain actionable insights and make informed decisions about optimizing your marketing strategies and tactics.

Stay Informed and Adapt:

Stay informed about emerging trends, best practices, and changes in social media algorithms and online marketing trends. Keep abreast of industry news, case studies, and success stories to learn from others and refine your approach.

Remain agile and adaptable in your social media and online marketing strategies, experimenting with new techniques, platforms, and technologies to stay ahead of the curve and maintain a competitive edge in the digital landscape.

Networking and Forming Partnerships for Business Growth

Readers are guided on the importance of networking and forming strategic partnerships as effective strategies for fostering business growth and expanding opportunities within their side hustle ventures. Networking involves building relationships, exchanging ideas, and creating connections with individuals and organizations that can offer support, resources, and collaboration opportunities. Here's how networking and forming partnerships are addressed in the book:

145

Identify Networking Opportunities:

Begin by identifying networking opportunities within your industry, niche, or local community where you can connect with like-minded individuals, entrepreneurs, professionals, and potential collaborators.

Attend industry events, conferences, workshops, seminars, meetups, and networking gatherings to expand your network and engage with peers who share similar interests, goals, or expertise.

Cultivate Meaningful Relationships:

Focus on cultivating genuine, meaningful relationships with individuals you meet through networking activities. Take the time to listen, learn, and understand their backgrounds, aspirations, and challenges.

Be authentic, approachable, and generous in your interactions, and seek opportunities to offer support, advice, or resources that can add value to their endeavors.

Leverage Digital Platforms:

Harness the power of digital platforms and online communities to expand your network and connect with a broader audience of potential partners, mentors, and collaborators.

Utilize social media platforms such as LinkedIn, Twitter, Facebook, and Instagram to showcase your expertise, share insights, and engage with industry influencers, thought leaders, and peers.

147

Participate in Professional Groups:

Join relevant professional associations, industry forums, and online groups where you can connect with professionals and entrepreneurs who share common interests or expertise.

Actively participate in group discussions, share valuable insights, and contribute to the community by offering advice, support, and solutions to fellow members.

Attend Networking Events:

Attend networking events specifically tailored to entrepreneurs, startups, and small business owners in your area. These events provide opportunities to meet potential partners, investors, mentors, and customers.

Be proactive in initiating conversations, exchanging contact information, and following up with individuals you meet to explore potential collaborations or business opportunities.

Seek Mentorship and Guidance:

Seek mentorship and guidance from experienced professionals, industry veterans, or successful entrepreneurs who can offer valuable advice, feedback, and mentorship to help you navigate the challenges and opportunities of entrepreneurship.

Look for mentors who have relevant experience, insights, and connections in your industry or field of interest. Be receptive to feedback, and leverage their expertise to accelerate your learning and growth.

Form Strategic Partnerships:

Explore opportunities to form strategic partnerships with complementary businesses, organizations, or individuals that share common goals, target audiences, or value propositions.

Collaborate on joint ventures, co-marketing campaigns, product launches, or events that leverage the strengths and resources of each partner to achieve mutual objectives and create win-win outcomes.

Nurture and Maintain Relationships:

Nuture and maintain relationships with your network over time by staying in touch, expressing gratitude, and offering support when needed. Keep your contacts informed about your progress, achievements, and new initiatives.

Regularly engage with your network through emails, phone calls, meetings, or social media interactions to reinforce connections and demonstrate your commitment to building meaningful relationships.

CHAPTER 7

OVERCOMING CHALLENGES AND OBSTACLES

Readers are equipped with strategies and insights to navigate the inevitable challenges and obstacles encountered on their journey towards side hustle success. While pursuing entrepreneurial endeavors during their spare time, individuals may encounter various hurdles that can test their resilience, creativity, and determination. Here's how overcoming challenges and obstacles is addressed in the book:

Embrace a Growth Mindset:

Encourage readers to adopt a growth mindset, viewing challenges and setbacks as opportunities for learning, growth, and self-improvement. Emphasize the importance of resilience, perseverance, and adaptability in overcoming obstacles and achieving success.

Identify Potential Challenges:

Help readers anticipate and identify potential challenges and obstacles that may arise in the course of their side hustle ventures. Common challenges may include time constraints, financial limitations, competition, market fluctuations, technical issues, and personal setbacks.

Develop Problem-Solving Skills:

Empower readers with problem-solving skills and strategies to effectively address and overcome challenges encountered along the way. Encourage creative thinking, resourcefulness, and flexibility in seeking solutions to complex problems and roadblocks.

Seek Support and Guidance:

Encourage readers to seek support, guidance, and mentorship from experienced professionals, peers, mentors, and support networks within their industry or community. Surrounding oneself with a supportive ecosystem can provide valuable insights, advice, and encouragement during challenging times.

Break Tasks into Manageable Steps:

Break down daunting tasks or projects into smaller, manageable steps that are easier to tackle and accomplish. By focusing on incremental progress and celebrating small victories, readers can maintain momentum and motivation in the face of adversity.

Stay Committed to Goals:

Remind readers of the importance of staying committed to their goals and maintaining a long-term perspective despite temporary setbacks or obstacles. Encourage persistence, determination, and consistency in pursuing their side hustle aspirations.

Learn from Setbacks:

Encourage readers to view setbacks and failures as valuable learning experiences that offer insights and lessons for future growth and improvement. Encourage reflection, self-assessment, and feedback-seeking to extract meaningful lessons from setbacks and apply them to future endeavors.

Stay Agile and Adapt:

Emphasize the importance of agility and adaptability in responding to changing circumstances, market

155

dynamics, and customer needs. Encourage readers to embrace change, experiment with new ideas, and pivot when necessary to stay relevant and competitive in their industries.

Cultivate Resilience:

Foster resilience by helping readers develop coping mechanisms, stress management techniques, and self-care practices to navigate challenges with confidence and composure. Encourage mindfulness, self-awareness, and balance in managing the demands of entrepreneurship and personal well-being.

Celebrate Progress:

Encourage readers to celebrate their progress, achievements, and milestones along the way, no matter how small. Recognize and acknowledge the hard work, dedication, and perseverance required to overcome challenges and make meaningful strides toward their goals.

By equipping readers with practical strategies, mindset shifts, and support systems for overcoming challenges and obstacles, "Weekend Side Hustle Techniques" empowers individuals to navigate the ups and downs of entrepreneurship with resilience, optimism, and determination. Through perseverance and a growth-oriented mindset, readers can transform challenges into opportunities for personal and professional growth, ultimately achieving success in their side hustle endeavors.

Addressing Common Challenges Faced by Side Hustlers

Readers are provided with insights and strategies to tackle common challenges encountered while navigating the landscape of side hustle entrepreneurship. Recognizing and addressing these challenges can empower individuals to overcome obstacles and thrive in their pursuit of additional income streams during their spare time. Here are some common challenges addressed in the book along with strategies to address them:

Time Constraints:

Challenge: Balancing full-time commitments with side hustle activities can pose significant time constraints, making it challenging to allocate sufficient time and energy to both responsibilities.

158

Strategy: Encourage readers to prioritize tasks, streamline processes, and leverage time management techniques to optimize their productivity and make the most of their available time. Setting realistic goals and establishing structured schedules can help individuals effectively manage their time and achieve balance between work and side hustle endeavors.

Financial Limitations:

Challenge: Limited financial resources may constrain individuals from investing in necessary tools, resources, or marketing efforts to grow their side hustle ventures.

Strategy: Provide readers with cost-effective strategies and creative solutions to bootstrap their side hustle ventures. Encourage them to focus on low-cost or no-cost marketing channels, leverage free

159

resources and platforms, and explore alternative funding options such as crowdfunding or bootstrapping. Emphasize the importance of financial planning, budgeting, and resource optimization to maximize the impact of limited financial resources.

Marketing and Promotion:

Challenge: Generating visibility and attracting customers or clients to their side hustle offerings can be a daunting task for many individuals.

Strategy: Equip readers with effective marketing and promotion strategies tailored to their target audience and niche market. Encourage them to leverage social media platforms, online marketplaces, and networking opportunities to amplify their reach and engage with potential customers. Provide guidance on crafting compelling messaging, storytelling, and branding strategies to differentiate their offerings and attract attention in competitive markets.

Skill Acquisition and Development:

Challenge: Acquiring and developing the necessary skills and expertise to succeed in their side hustle ventures may present a steep learning curve for individuals entering new industries or pursuing unfamiliar business models.

Strategy: Encourage continuous learning, skill development, and self-improvement through online courses, workshops, mentorship programs, and industry events. Provide readers with resources and recommendations for accessing relevant educational materials, acquiring new skills, and staying abreast of industry trends and best practices. Foster a growth mindset and a commitment to lifelong learning as essential components of entrepreneurial success.

Work-Life Balance:

Challenge: Maintaining a healthy work-life balance while juggling multiple responsibilities and commitments can be challenging for side hustlers.

Strategy: Emphasize the importance of setting boundaries, prioritizing self-care, and allocating time for rest, relaxation, and personal fulfillment. Encourage readers to establish clear boundaries between work and personal life, delegate tasks when possible, and practice effective stress management techniques to prevent burnout and maintain overall well-being.

Competition and Market Saturation:

Challenge: Navigating competitive markets and standing out amidst saturation can pose significant challenges for side hustle entrepreneurs.

Strategy: Encourage readers to differentiate their offerings by identifying unique value propositions, niche markets, or underserved customer segments. Emphasize the importance of authenticity, storytelling, and building genuine connections with customers to foster loyalty and trust. Encourage continuous innovation, adaptability, and responsiveness to market feedback to stay ahead of competitors and capitalize on emerging opportunities.

Strategies for Managing Stress and Burnout

Readers are provided with practical strategies and techniques to effectively manage stress and prevent burnout while pursuing their side hustle endeavors. Recognizing the demands and pressures associated with balancing full-time commitments and entrepreneurial pursuits, the book emphasizes the importance of self-care, resilience, and stress management to maintain overall well-being and sustain long-term success. Here are some strategies for managing stress and burnout addressed in the book:

Prioritize Self-Care:

Encourage readers to prioritize self-care practices to nurture their physical, mental, and emotional health. Emphasize the importance of adequate sleep, nutritious eating habits, regular exercise, and relaxation techniques such as meditation, yoga, or deep breathing exercises.

Set Boundaries:

Encourage readers to establish clear boundaries between work, side hustle activities, and personal life. Define designated times for work and relaxation, and resist the temptation to constantly be "on" or available. Communicate boundaries with clients, customers, and colleagues to prevent overextension and burnout.

Practice Time Management:

Provide readers with time management strategies to effectively allocate their time and prioritize tasks. Encourage the use of productivity tools, such as calendars, to-do lists, and time-blocking techniques, to optimize workflow and minimize stress from feeling

165

overwhelmed by competing demands.

Delegate and Outsource:

Encourage readers to delegate tasks and responsibilities when feasible, both in their full-time roles and side hustle ventures. Consider outsourcing non-core activities or tasks that are outside of one's expertise to free up time and mental bandwidth for more impactful and fulfilling endeavors.

Learn to Say No:

Empower readers to set boundaries and assertively say no to commitments, projects, or opportunities that do not align with their priorities or values. Encourage them to focus on activities that contribute to their overall goals and well-being, rather than spreading themselves too thin.

Practice Mindfulness:

Introduce mindfulness practices to help readers cultivate present-moment awareness and reduce stress levels. Encourage mindfulness meditation, mindful breathing exercises, or mindful eating practices to foster relaxation, clarity, and resilience in the face of challenges.

Seek Social Support:

Encourage readers to seek support from friends, family members, mentors, and peers during times of stress or overwhelm. Foster a sense of community and belonging by engaging in meaningful connections, sharing experiences, and seeking advice or encouragement from trusted individuals.

Schedule Regular Breaks:

Remind readers of the importance of taking regular breaks throughout the day to recharge and rejuvenate. Encourage short breaks for stretching, walking, or engaging in hobbies to break up periods of intense focus and prevent mental fatigue.

Foster Work-Life Integration:

Encourage readers to embrace a holistic approach to work-life balance, where work and personal life are integrated harmoniously to support overall well-being. Encourage them to find joy and fulfillment in both professional and personal pursuits, and strive for a sense of balance and alignment in their daily lives.

Monitor Stress Levels:

Encourage readers to monitor their stress levels and recognize early warning signs of burnout, such as fatigue, irritability, or decreased motivation. Encourage proactive measures to address stress, such as seeking professional support, adjusting workload, or reassessing priorities.

Learning from Failures and Adapting to Setbacks

Readers are encouraged to embrace failures as valuable learning experiences and to adapt to setbacks as opportunities for growth and improvement. Recognizing that setbacks are an inevitable part of the entrepreneurial journey, the book emphasizes the importance of resilience, flexibility, and a growth mindset in navigating challenges and achieving success in side hustle ventures. Here's how learning from failures and adapting to setbacks are addressed in the book:

Embrace Failure as a Learning Opportunity:

Encourage readers to reframe their perspective on failure and view it as a natural and necessary part of the learning process. Emphasize that failures provide valuable insights, feedback, and opportunities for reflection and growth.

Encourage readers to adopt a mindset of curiosity and resilience, and to approach setbacks with a willingness to learn from their experiences and adapt their strategies accordingly.

Analyze and Reflect on Failures:

Encourage readers to analyze and reflect on their failures in a constructive and objective manner. Prompt them to identify the root causes of the failure, evaluate the decisions and actions that led to the outcome, and consider alternative approaches or solutions.

Encourage readers to view failures as data points that inform their future decisions and strategies, rather than as indicators of personal inadequacy or incompetence.

Extract Lessons and Insights:

Guide readers to extract meaningful lessons and insights from their failures that can inform their approach to future endeavors. Encourage them to identify patterns, trends, or recurring themes in their failures, and to discern actionable takeaways that can inform their decision-making and problem-solving processes.

Emphasize the importance of humility and open-mindedness in acknowledging mistakes, seeking feedback, and incorporating lessons learned into their ongoing efforts.

171

Cultivate Adaptability and Resilience:

Encourage readers to cultivate adaptability and resilience in response to setbacks and unforeseen challenges. Highlight the importance of flexibility, resourcefulness, and the ability to pivot in changing circumstances.

Encourage readers to develop coping mechanisms, stress management techniques, and support networks that help them navigate adversity with grace and perseverance.

Iterate and Experiment:

Encourage readers to adopt an iterative approach to their side hustle ventures, embracing experimentation and refinement as core principles of entrepreneurship. Encourage them to test hypotheses, iterate on their ideas, and adapt their strategies based on real-world feedback and outcomes.

Foster a culture of experimentation, creativity, and innovation, where failures are viewed as stepping stones to success rather than deterrents to progress.

Celebrate Progress and Small Wins:

Encourage readers to celebrate their progress and small wins along the way, even in the face of setbacks and challenges. Highlight the importance of acknowledging milestones, achievements, and incremental improvements as markers of progress and resilience.

Foster a sense of optimism, gratitude, and positivity by recognizing and celebrating the efforts and achievements of readers

173

as they navigate the ups and downs of their entrepreneurial journey.

By encouraging readers to embrace failures as opportunities for growth, learn from setbacks, and adapt their strategies accordingly, "Weekend Side Hustle Techniques" empowers individuals to cultivate resilience, creativity, and perseverance in pursuing their side hustle aspirations. Through a combination of reflection, adaptation, and continuous learning, readers can transform setbacks into stepping stones toward success and fulfillment in their entrepreneurial endeavors.

CHAPTER 8

LEGAL AND REGULATORY CONSIDERATIONS

Readers are introduced to essential legal and regulatory considerations to ensure compliance and mitigate potential risks associated with their side hustle ventures. Understanding the legal landscape and adhering to applicable regulations is crucial for safeguarding the integrity of the business and protecting the interests of both entrepreneurs and their customers. Here are key legal and regulatory considerations addressed in the book:

Business Structure:

Guide readers in selecting an appropriate business structure for their side hustle ventures, such as

175

sole proprietorship, partnership, limited liability company (LLC), or corporation. Explain the advantages and disadvantages of each structure in terms of liability protection, tax implications, and administrative requirements.

Registration and Licensing:

Educate readers about the importance of registering their businesses and obtaining the necessary licenses and permits required to operate legally in their jurisdiction. Provide guidance on the specific registration and licensing requirements applicable to their industry, location, and type of business activity.

Tax Obligations:

Highlight the importance of understanding tax obligations and compliance requirements associated with running a side hustle business.

Explain the implications of different tax structures, filing deadlines, deductible expenses, and record-keeping practices to ensure accurate reporting and compliance with tax laws.

Intellectual Property Protection:

Raise awareness about the importance of protecting intellectual property assets, such as trademarks, copyrights, patents, and trade secrets, associated with their side hustle ventures. Educate readers on the process of securing intellectual property rights and enforcing protections against infringement or unauthorized use.

Contractual Agreements:

Provide guidance on drafting and negotiating contractual agreements, such as client contracts, service agreements, vendor contracts, and partnership agreements, to formalize business relationships and clarify rights and obligations. Emphasize the importance of clear, concise, and enforceable contract terms to mitigate disputes and liabilities.

Data Privacy and Security:

Inform readers about the importance of safeguarding customer data and complying with data privacy regulations, such as the General Data Protection Regulation (GDPR) or the California Consumer Privacy Act (CCPA). Offer guidance on implementing data privacy policies, secure data storage practices, and protocols for handling sensitive information.

Compliance with Industry Regulations:

Educate readers about industry-specific regulations and compliance requirements that may impact their side hustle ventures, such as food safety regulations for culinary businesses, health and safety standards for wellness services, or licensing requirements for professional services. Provide resources and references for staying informed about evolving regulatory changes and best practices.

Liability Protection:

Discuss strategies for mitigating liability risks associated with side hustle activities, such as obtaining liability insurance coverage, implementing risk management protocols, and adhering to industry standards and best practices. Highlight the importance of separating personal and business assets to shield personal finances from potential liabilities.

Dispute Resolution:

Introduce readers to alternative dispute resolution mechanisms, such

179

as mediation or arbitration, as cost-effective and efficient alternatives to traditional litigation for resolving disputes and conflicts that may arise in the course of their side hustle ventures.

Understanding Legal Requirements for Side Businesses

Readers gain insight into the crucial legal requirements and considerations necessary for operating side businesses. Recognizing the significance of compliance and adherence to legal standards, the book educates individuals on the following key aspects:

Business Structure Selection:

Readers are guided through the process of selecting an appropriate business structure for their side businesses, such as sole proprietorship, partnership, limited liability company (LLC), or corporation. Each structure carries distinct implications for liability, taxation, and administrative obligations, which readers learn to evaluate based on their specific needs and circumstances.

Registration and Licensing:

The book emphasizes the importance of registering side businesses and obtaining necessary licenses and permits to operate legally. Readers are informed about the specific requirements dictated by their industry, location, and business activities, ensuring compliance with regulatory standards and avoiding potential penalties.

Taxation and Financial Obligations:

Understanding tax obligations is paramount for side business owners. The book provides clarity on tax implications associated with different business structures and revenue streams. Readers learn about tax filing requirements, deductible expenses, and record-keeping practices to maintain accurate financial records and comply with tax laws.

Intellectual Property Protection:

Intellectual property (IP) protection is addressed to safeguard side business assets such as trademarks, copyrights, patents, and trade secrets. Readers are educated on the importance of securing IP rights and enforcing protections against infringement, enhancing the value and integrity of their brands and innovations.

Contractual Agreements:

Guidance is provided on drafting, negotiating, and executing contractual agreements essential for side business operations. Readers learn to formalize relationships with clients, vendors, partners, and employees through clear and enforceable contracts, mitigating risks and clarifying rights and responsibilities.

Data Privacy and Security:

In an era of heightened data privacy concerns, readers are instructed on the importance of protecting customer data and adhering to data privacy regulations. The book introduces best practices for implementing data privacy policies, secure data storage methods, and protocols for handling sensitive information, ensuring compliance with legal standards and maintaining customer trust.

Compliance with Industry Regulations:

Industry-specific regulations and compliance requirements are explored to address unique considerations relevant to various side business ventures. Readers gain insights into sector-specific regulations such as food safety standards, healthcare regulations, or professional licensing requirements, ensuring adherence to industry norms and legal standards.

Liability Protection:

Mitigating liability risks is essential for safeguarding personal and business assets. The book educates readers on strategies for minimizing exposure to legal liabilities, including obtaining liability insurance coverage, implementing risk management protocols, and maintaining separation between personal and business finances.

Registering a Business Entity and Obtaining Necessary Licenses

Readers are guided through the process of registering a business entity and obtaining the necessary licenses and permits essential for operating their side businesses legally and effectively. Understanding the importance of compliance and adherence to regulatory requirements, the book provides actionable steps and insights to navigate the following key aspects:

Choosing a Business Structure:

Readers are introduced to different business structures, including sole proprietorship, partnership, limited liability company (LLC), and corporation. They learn about the unique characteristics, advantages, and disadvantages of each structure, enabling them to make informed decisions based on their specific needs, goals, and preferences.

Business Name Registration:

The book emphasizes the significance of choosing a unique and memorable business name that aligns with the brand identity and target market. Readers learn about the process of registering their business name with the appropriate government authorities, ensuring legal protection and exclusivity.

Entity Registration:

Step-by-step guidance is provided on the process of registering the chosen business entity with the relevant state or local government agencies.

Readers learn about the required documentation, fees, and procedures involved in formalizing their business structure and establishing legal recognition.

Obtaining Licenses and Permits:

Readers are educated about the specific licenses, permits, and certifications required to conduct their side business activities lawfully. They gain insights into industry-specific regulations and compliance requirements, ensuring adherence to legal standards and avoiding potential penalties or liabilities.

Researching Regulatory Requirements:

The book emphasizes the importance of conducting thorough research to identify and understand the regulatory landscape governing their particular industry or business

187

activities. Readers learn to navigate regulatory websites, consult with industry associations, and seek professional advice to ensure comprehensive compliance with applicable laws and regulations.

Compliance Checklist:

A comprehensive compliance checklist is provided to assist readers in systematically addressing and fulfilling the necessary legal and regulatory requirements for their side businesses. From tax registration to health and safety permits, readers gain clarity on the essential elements of regulatory compliance and are empowered to proactively address potential areas of concern.

Renewal and Maintenance:

Readers are reminded of the importance of ongoing compliance and maintenance of their business registrations, licenses, and permits.

They learn about renewal deadlines, reporting requirements, and other obligations necessary to sustain legal recognition and operational continuity.

Complying with Tax Regulations and Financial Reporting Obligations

Readers are provided with essential guidance on complying with tax regulations and fulfilling financial reporting obligations associated with their side hustle ventures. Understanding the importance of financial transparency, accountability, and compliance, the book offers actionable strategies and insights to navigate the following key aspects:

Understanding Tax Obligations:

Readers are educated about the various tax obligations relevant to their side businesses, including income taxes, sales taxes, and self-employment taxes. They learn about the tax implications associated with different business structures and revenue streams, enabling them to make informed decisions regarding tax planning and compliance.

Registering for Tax Identification Numbers:

The book guides readers through the process of obtaining the necessary tax identification numbers, such as Employer Identification Numbers (EINs) or state tax identification numbers, required for tax reporting and compliance purposes. Readers learn about the application procedures and documentation requirements involved in securing these identifiers.

Maintaining Accurate Financial Records:

Emphasizing the importance of maintaining accurate and organized financial records, readers are provided with practical tips and tools for record-keeping. They learn about the essential financial documents, such as income statements, expense reports, and balance sheets, necessary for tracking business transactions and preparing tax returns.

Tracking Business Expenses:

Readers are encouraged to diligently track and categorize their business expenses to maximize tax deductions and minimize taxable income. They learn about allowable business deductions, including expenses related to supplies, equipment, advertising, travel, and home office expenses, ensuring they

191

capture all eligible deductions while preparing their tax returns.

Filing Tax Returns:

Step-by-step guidance is provided on the process of filing tax returns for side businesses, including individual tax returns (Form 1040) and business tax returns (such as Schedule C for sole proprietors or Form 1065 for partnerships). Readers learn about filing deadlines, payment methods, and electronic filing options available to streamline the tax filing process.

Understanding Quarterly Estimated Taxes:

For side hustlers with fluctuating income or self-employment earnings, the book explains the concept of quarterly estimated taxes and the importance of making timely and accurate tax payments throughout the year. Readers learn about the calculation methods, due dates, and penalty implications associated with underpayment of estimated taxes.

Seeking Professional Tax Advice:

Recognizing the complexity of tax laws and regulations, readers are encouraged to seek professional tax advice from qualified tax professionals, accountants, or tax preparers. They learn about the benefits of working with tax professionals to navigate tax planning, compliance, and audit defense strategies tailored to their specific business needs.

Maintaining Compliance with Reporting Obligations:

The book highlights the importance of compliance with financial reporting obligations imposed by regulatory authorities and governing bodies. Readers are educated about the reporting requirements for business income, expenses, assets, liabilities, and other financial metrics essential for regulatory compliance and transparency.

CHAPTER 9

SCALING YOUR SIDE HUSTLE

In "Weekend Side Hustle Techniques: After 5 to 9, How to Make Money on the Side in Your Spare Time," readers are provided with valuable insights and strategies for scaling their side hustles to achieve growth, sustainability, and long-term success. Recognizing the potential for expansion and diversification within side businesses, the book offers actionable steps and practical advice on the following key aspects of scaling:

Assessing Growth Opportunities: Readers are encouraged to conduct a comprehensive assessment of growth opportunities within their side hustle ventures. They learn to identify market trends, customer needs, and competitive advantages that can serve as catalysts for expansion and scalability.

Setting Clear Goals and Objectives:

The book emphasizes the importance of setting clear, measurable, and achievable goals and objectives for scaling their side hustles. Readers learn to establish key performance indicators (KPIs) and milestones to track progress and evaluate the success of their growth initiatives.

Streamlining Processes and Workflows:

Efficiency and productivity are prioritized as readers are guided to streamline processes and workflows within their side hustle operations. They learn to identify inefficiencies, automate repetitive tasks, and optimize resource allocation to enhance scalability and performance.

Investing in Infrastructure and Resources:

Readers are encouraged to invest in the necessary infrastructure, technologies, and resources to support their scaling efforts. Whether it's upgrading equipment, expanding production capacity, or hiring additional staff, they learn to strategically allocate resources to accommodate growth and demand.

Expanding Product or Service Offerings:

Diversification is explored as readers are encouraged to expand their product or service offerings to appeal to a broader customer base or capitalize on emerging market trends. They learn to innovate, iterate, and introduce new products or services that complement their

197

existing offerings and address evolving customer needs.

Leveraging Digital Marketing and E-commerce:

The book highlights the importance of leveraging digital marketing channels and e-commerce platforms to reach a wider audience and drive growth for their side hustles. Readers learn about content marketing, social media advertising, search engine optimization (SEO), and other digital strategies to enhance visibility, engagement, and conversion rates.

Building Strategic Partnerships:

Collaboration and partnership are encouraged as readers explore opportunities to form strategic alliances with complementary businesses, influencers, or organizations. They learn to leverage partnerships for joint marketing campaigns, co-branded initiatives, and shared resources to accelerate growth and expansion.

Cultivating Customer Loyalty and Advocacy:

Readers are reminded of the significance of customer retention and advocacy in sustaining growth for their side hustle ventures. They learn to prioritize customer satisfaction, feedback, and engagement to foster long-term relationships and build a loyal customer base that drives recurring revenue and referrals.

Monitoring and Adjusting Strategies:

Continuous monitoring and evaluation are emphasized as readers track the performance of their scaling efforts and adjust strategies as needed. They learn to gather feedback, analyze data, and

199

adapt to changing market conditions to optimize outcomes and maximize return on investment (ROI).

Strategies for Expanding and Diversifying Side Hustle Ventures

Readers are introduced to effective strategies for expanding and diversifying their side hustle ventures. Recognizing the potential for growth and scalability, the book offers actionable insights and approaches to capitalize on emerging opportunities and maximize the impact of side hustle endeavors. Here are key strategies for expanding and diversifying side hustle ventures addressed in the book:

Market Research and Analysis: Encourage readers to conduct thorough market research and

200

analysis to identify untapped opportunities, emerging trends, and customer needs within their target markets. By gaining insights into market dynamics, competitive landscapes, and consumer preferences, readers can uncover potential niches and avenues for expansion.

Product and Service Innovation:

Inspire readers to innovate and diversify their offerings by introducing new products, services, or variations tailored to evolving customer demands and market trends. Encourage experimentation, creativity, and feedback-driven iteration to refine existing offerings and explore new revenue streams.

Scaling Operations:

Guide readers in developing scalable business models and operational processes that can accommodate increased demand and growth. Encourage the adoption of efficient workflows, automation tools, and outsourcing strategies to streamline operations and optimize resource utilization.

Strategic Partnerships and Collaborations:

Advocate for strategic partnerships and collaborations with complementary businesses, influencers, or industry leaders to amplify reach, access new markets, and leverage existing networks. Encourage readers to explore mutually beneficial partnerships that enhance brand visibility, credibility, and market penetration.

Geographic Expansion:

Explore opportunities for geographic expansion by targeting new geographic regions, markets, or demographics beyond existing territories. Provide guidance on market entry strategies, localization efforts, and cultural considerations to effectively penetrate and establish footholds in new markets.

Diversification of Revenue Streams:

Encourage readers to diversify their revenue streams by exploring multiple income sources, such as product sales, service offerings, affiliate marketing, licensing agreements, or digital products. By diversifying revenue streams, readers can mitigate risks and capitalize on diverse income opportunities.

Customer Relationship Management:

Emphasize the importance of building strong customer relationships and fostering customer loyalty through personalized experiences, exceptional service, and responsive communication. Encourage readers to solicit feedback, address customer needs, and nurture long-term relationships to drive repeat business and referrals.

Brand Building and Marketing:

Guide readers in building a strong brand identity and cohesive marketing strategy that resonates with their target audience and distinguishes their offerings in competitive markets. Encourage the use of storytelling, visual branding, and digital marketing channels to engage customers and amplify brand awareness.

Continuous Learning and Adaptation:

Foster a culture of continuous learning, adaptability, and experimentation among readers,

204

encouraging them to stay abreast of industry trends, consumer behaviors, and technological innovations. Emphasize the importance of agility, resilience, and a growth mindset in navigating changing market dynamics and seizing opportunities for growth.

Financial Planning and Resource Allocation:

Advocate for prudent financial planning and resource allocation to support expansion and diversification efforts. Encourage readers to assess investment opportunities, manage cash flow, and prioritize expenditures to optimize returns and sustain long-term growth.

Hiring Assistance and Delegating Tasks as the Business Grows

Readers are introduced to the importance of hiring assistance and delegating tasks as their side hustle ventures expand and evolve. Recognizing the limitations of time and resources, the book offers practical insights and strategies for effectively leveraging support to scale operations and sustain growth. Here are key considerations for hiring assistance and delegating tasks addressed in the book:

Assessing Workload and Capacity:

Encourage readers to conduct a thorough assessment of their workload, priorities, and available resources to determine the need for additional assistance. By evaluating the scope and complexity of tasks, readers can identify areas where delegation or hiring support would be most beneficial.

Identifying Core Competencies and Skill Gaps:

Guide readers in identifying their core competencies, strengths, and areas of expertise, as well as potential skill gaps or areas where additional expertise is needed. Encourage honest self-assessment and reflection to pinpoint tasks or responsibilities that could be outsourced or delegated to others.

Defining Roles and Responsibilities:

Emphasize the importance of defining clear roles, responsibilities, and expectations for hired assistance or team members. Encourage readers to articulate specific tasks, deadlines, and

207

performance metrics to ensure alignment and accountability in delegated assignments.

Hiring Freelancers, Contractors, or Virtual Assistants:

Introduce readers to the concept of hiring freelancers, contractors, or virtual assistants to fulfill specific tasks or projects on a temporary or part-time basis. Provide guidance on sourcing and vetting candidates, negotiating agreements, and establishing effective communication channels for remote collaboration.

Outsourcing Non-Core Functions:

Advocate for outsourcing non-core functions or repetitive tasks that do not require specialized expertise or direct oversight. Encourage readers to prioritize their time and energy on high-impact activities that align with

208

their strengths and strategic objectives, while delegating routine tasks to capable assistants.

Leveraging Technology and Automation:

Highlight the role of technology and automation tools in streamlining workflows, optimizing productivity, and reducing manual labor. Introduce readers to software solutions, productivity apps, and project management platforms that can facilitate task delegation, communication, and collaboration among team members.

Providing Training and Support:

Stress the importance of providing adequate training, guidance, and support to hired assistance or team members to ensure their success and integration into the business. Encourage readers to invest in professional development opportunities, mentorship, and ongoing feedback to foster a culture of continuous learning and improvement.

Monitoring Performance and Results:

Encourage readers to establish mechanisms for monitoring performance, tracking results, and evaluating the effectiveness of delegated tasks or projects. Emphasize the importance of regular feedback sessions, performance reviews, and key performance indicators (KPIs) to assess progress and identify areas for optimization.

Cultivating a Collaborative Culture:

Foster a collaborative and inclusive culture within the organization, where team members feel valued, empowered, and motivated to contribute their skills and ideas.

210

Encourage open communication, transparency, and a shared sense of purpose to foster a positive work environment conducive to growth and innovation.

Maintaining Work-Life Balance While Scaling Operations

Maintaining work-life balance is emphasized as a critical aspect, especially when scaling side hustle operations. As individuals strive to expand their ventures while managing other commitments, it's essential to prioritize balance and well-being. Here are strategies outlined in the book for achieving this balance:

Setting Clear Boundaries:

Encourage readers to establish clear boundaries between work and personal life, defining specific times for side hustle activities and dedicated periods for relaxation, family time, and self-care. Emphasize the importance of respecting these boundaries to prevent burnout and maintain overall well-being.

Prioritizing Tasks and Responsibilities:

Guide readers in prioritizing tasks and responsibilities based on importance and urgency, focusing on high-impact activities that align with strategic objectives while delegating or postponing less critical tasks. Help readers identify time-sensitive deadlines and allocate sufficient time for essential activities without sacrificing personal time.

Embracing Time Management Techniques:

Introduce readers to effective time management techniques, such as the Pomodoro Technique, time blocking,

212

and prioritization methods, to optimize productivity and balance competing demands. Encourage readers to allocate dedicated blocks of time for focused work, breaks, and leisure activities to maintain energy and concentration levels.

Automating and Streamlining Processes:

Advocate for the automation and streamlining of routine tasks and processes to minimize manual labor and free up time for more meaningful activities. Introduce readers to productivity tools, project management software, and automation solutions that can simplify workflows and improve efficiency in side hustle operations.

Outsourcing Non-Core Functions:

Encourage readers to outsource non-core functions or repetitive tasks that consume valuable time and energy, allowing them to focus on high-value activities that drive business growth. Discuss the benefits of hiring freelancers, virtual assistants, or contractors to handle administrative, marketing, or operational tasks as the business scales.

Communicating Expectations Effectively:

Stress the importance of effective communication in setting expectations with clients, collaborators, and team members regarding availability, response times, and project timelines. Encourage transparent communication about workload, capacity, and boundaries to manage expectations and avoid overcommitment.

Practicing Self-Care and Well-Being:

Remind readers to prioritize self-care and well-being amidst the demands of scaling side hustle operations. Encourage regular exercise, healthy eating habits, sufficient sleep, and stress-reduction techniques to maintain physical and mental health. Emphasize the importance of setting aside time for hobbies, relaxation, and rejuvenation to replenish energy and prevent burnout.

Seeking Support and Delegating Responsibilities:

Encourage readers to seek support from friends, family members, or support networks to share responsibilities and provide emotional support during busy periods. Empower readers to delegate tasks, ask for help when needed, and collaborate with trusted

partners to distribute workload and prevent overwhelm.

CHAPTER 10
CONCLUSION: EMBRACING THE JOURNEY OF FINANCIAL EMPOWERMENT

As readers conclude their journey through "Weekend Side Hustle Techniques: After 5 to 9, How to Make Money on the Side in Your Spare Time," it's essential to reflect on the transformative power of leveraging spare time for financial empowerment. Throughout this book, we have explored a multitude of strategies, insights, and practical techniques aimed at helping individuals unlock their full potential and achieve greater financial independence.

At the heart of every side hustle venture lies the spirit of entrepreneurship the relentless pursuit of opportunity, innovation, and self-reliance. We have witnessed how spare time side hustles serve as catalysts for personal and professional growth, providing avenues for creativity, exploration, and self-discovery beyond the confines of traditional employment.

From identifying marketable skills and interests to exploring diverse revenue streams, readers have embarked on a journey of self-exploration and empowerment, uncovering hidden talents, passions, and opportunities along the way. We have delved into the nuances of time management, productivity, and balance, recognizing the importance of prioritizing well-being and fulfillment amidst the demands of scaling operations.

Through the ups and downs, successes and setbacks, readers have embraced the entrepreneurial mindset – a mindset characterized by resilience, adaptability, and unwavering determination. We have celebrated the victories, learned from the challenges, and embraced the iterative process of growth and learning inherent in the entrepreneurial journey.

As we bid farewell to this book, let us carry forward the lessons learned and the insights gained into our future endeavors. Let us continue to embrace the spirit of innovation, collaboration, and continuous improvement as we navigate the ever-changing landscape of entrepreneurship and beyond.

Above all, let us remember that the pursuit of financial empowerment is not merely about accumulating wealth or achieving success it is about reclaiming control of our destinies, fulfilling our potential, and making a meaningful impact in the world around us. Whether we are starting small or dreaming big, every step forward is a testament to our resilience, ambition, and belief in the power of possibility.

As we venture forth into the world of side hustles and beyond, may we always remember the words of wisdom, encouragement, and inspiration shared within these pages. May we dare to dream, strive for excellence, and embrace the journey with courage, curiosity, and unwavering resolve.

Recap of Key Insights and Strategies

Understanding Side Hustles:
The book begins by defining side hustles as entrepreneurial endeavors pursued outside of traditional employment, highlighting their

potential for additional income generation and personal fulfillment.

Identifying Skills and Interests:
Readers are encouraged to explore their skills, interests, and passions to uncover potential side hustle opportunities aligned with their strengths and preferences.

Market Research and Validation:
Conducting thorough market research and validation is emphasized to identify viable business ideas, assess market demand, and evaluate competition before investing time and resources.

Diversifying Revenue Streams:
The importance of diversifying revenue streams is highlighted, encouraging readers to explore multiple income sources, such as product sales, services, affiliate marketing, and digital products.

Time Management and Productivity:

Strategies for effective time management and productivity are discussed, including prioritization techniques, time blocking, and leveraging productivity tools to optimize workflow efficiency.

Scaling Operations:

As side hustle ventures grow, readers are advised to scale operations strategically by outsourcing non-core tasks, automating processes, and leveraging technology to accommodate increased demand.

Financial Planning and Management:

Readers learn about the significance of financial planning and management, including budgeting, expense tracking, tax compliance, and investment strategies to ensure long-term financial stability.

Marketing and Promotion:

Effective marketing and promotion strategies are explored, emphasizing the importance of building a personal brand, utilizing social media channels, networking, and forming partnerships to reach target audiences and drive sales.

Work-Life Balance:

Maintaining work-life balance is emphasized throughout the book, with strategies provided to prevent burnout, set boundaries, prioritize self-care, and allocate time for personal interests and relationships.

Overcoming Challenges and Setbacks:

Readers are encouraged to embrace challenges and setbacks as opportunities for growth, learning, and resilience-building, fostering a mindset of perseverance and adaptability in the face of adversity.

Legal and Regulatory Considerations:

Legal and regulatory considerations are discussed, including business registration, obtaining licenses and permits, tax compliance, and intellectual property protection to ensure legal and ethical business operations.

Continuous Learning and Adaptation:

The importance of continuous learning, adaptation, and staying abreast of industry trends and technological advancements is highlighted, empowering readers to remain agile and competitive in evolving market landscapes.

Encouragement for Readers to Take Action and Pursue Their Side Hustle Goals

As you journey through the pages of "Weekend Side Hustle Techniques: After 5 to 9, How to Make Money on the Side in Your Spare Time," I want to take a moment to share some words of encouragement and empowerment with you.

You hold in your hands a guide filled with insights, strategies, and practical advice aimed at unlocking the full potential of your spare time and propelling you towards your side hustle goals. But remember, the power to transform your aspirations into reality lies within you.

Now is the time to take action, to embrace the possibilities that await you beyond the confines of your regular 9-to-5 routine. It's time to

225

harness the untapped potential of your skills, passions, and creativity to carve out your path to financial independence and personal fulfillment.

I encourage you to believe in yourself, to trust in your abilities, and to dare to dream big. Your side hustle journey may be filled with challenges and uncertainties, but remember that every obstacle is an opportunity in disguise, every setback a chance to learn and grow stronger.

Don't wait for the perfect moment or the ideal circumstances to begin. Start where you are, with what you have, and let your journey unfold one step at a time. Embrace the process, celebrate your progress, and never lose sight of the vision that fuels your ambition.

As you embark on this journey, remember that you are not alone. Draw inspiration from the stories of those who have walked this path before you, seek guidance from mentors and peers, and surround yourself with a community of support that uplifts and encourages you along the way.

Be bold in your pursuits, resilient in the face of adversity, and relentless in your commitment to turning your dreams into reality. Remember that success is not measured by the destination alone but by the courage, determination, and perseverance you demonstrate along the way.

So, I urge you to take that first step, to seize this moment and embark on your side hustle journey with passion, purpose, and unwavering resolve. Believe in the extraordinary potential that lies within you, and let your journey of empowerment and self-discovery begin.

Your time is now. Your dreams are within reach. Let nothing hold you back from pursuing the life you envision and deserve.

With boundless optimism and unwavering belief in your potential,

Final Thoughts on the Significance of Leveraging Spare Time for Financial Empowerment

The journey towards financial empowerment through the utilization of spare time is not just a practical endeavor but also a transformative one. As readers conclude their exploration of side hustle techniques and strategies, it's essential to reflect on the broader significance of this pursuit. Here are final thoughts encapsulating the importance of leveraging spare time for financial empowerment:

Seizing Control of Personal Finances:

By engaging in side hustle ventures during their spare time, individuals take proactive steps towards gaining greater control over their financial destinies. They recognize the power of self-reliance and entrepreneurship in shaping their financial futures, breaking free from the constraints of traditional employment and embracing opportunities for growth and autonomy.

Unlocking Potential and Creativity:

Leveraging spare time for financial empowerment encourages individuals to tap into their innate talents, passions, and creativity. It fosters a culture of innovation, experimentation, and continuous

229

learning, where individuals are encouraged to explore new ideas, take calculated risks, and push the boundaries of what's possible.

Building Resilience and Adaptability:

The pursuit of financial empowerment through side hustle endeavors instills resilience and adaptability in individuals, preparing them to navigate the uncertainties and challenges of the modern economy. It cultivates a mindset of resourcefulness, problem-solving, and perseverance, empowering individuals to overcome obstacles and thrive in the face of adversity.

Creating Opportunities for Growth and Development:

Spare time side hustles serve as catalysts for personal and professional growth, providing opportunities for skill development, networking, and self-discovery. They offer avenues for individuals to explore new interests, expand their knowledge base, and cultivate valuable experiences that enrich their lives beyond monetary rewards.

Fostering a Culture of Financial Literacy and Independence:

Engaging in side hustle activities encourages individuals to become more financially literate and independent, equipping them with the knowledge, skills, and confidence to make informed decisions about money management and wealth creation. It promotes a culture of financial empowerment, where individuals take ownership of their financial well-being and advocate for economic self-sufficiency.

Redefining Work-Life Balance:

Embracing side hustles in spare time redefines the concept of work-life balance, challenging traditional notions of employment and productivity. It encourages individuals to pursue passions, interests, and aspirations outside of their primary careers, fostering a more holistic and fulfilling approach to life and livelihood.

Empowering Future Generations:

The pursuit of financial empowerment through spare time side hustles sets a powerful example for future generations, inspiring them to embrace entrepreneurship, innovation, and self-determination as pathways to success. It instills values of resilience, initiative, and ambition, shaping a legacy of empowerment and opportunity for generations to come.